What We Owe to Future People

What We Owe to Future People

A Contractualist Account of Intergenerational Ethics

ELIZABETH FINNERON-BURNS

OXFORD
UNIVERSITY PRESS

Oxford University Press is a department of the University of Oxford. It furthers the University's objective of excellence in research, scholarship, and education by publishing worldwide. Oxford is a registered trade mark of Oxford University Press in the UK and certain other countries.

Published in the United States of America by Oxford University Press
198 Madison Avenue, New York, NY 10016, United States of America.

© Oxford University Press 2024

All rights reserved. No part of this publication may be reproduced, stored in a retrieval system, or transmitted, in any form or by any means, without the prior permission in writing of Oxford University Press, or as expressly permitted by law, by license, or under terms agreed with the appropriate reproduction rights organization. Inquiries concerning reproduction outside the scope of the above should be sent to the Rights Department, Oxford University Press, at the address above.

You must not circulate this work in any other form
and you must impose this same condition on any acquirer.

Library of Congress Control Number: 2023051077

ISBN 978-0-19-765325-8

DOI: 10.1093/oso/9780197653258.001.0001

Printed by Integrated Books International, United States of America

For Baba

Contents

Acknowledgements ix

A 'Mind-Bending Topic' 1

1. Contractualism(s) 15

2. Justification to Future People 55

3. Intergenerational Resource Distribution 88

4. Permissible Procreation 121

5. Optimal Population Size 140

6. Our Future Is Uncertain 167

7. What *Do* We Owe to Future People? 183

8. Conclusion 199

Bibliography 207
Index 215

Acknowledgements

First and foremost, I want to thank T. M. Scanlon, who has no idea who I am, but who wrote the book that has captured my interest for over 15 years and from which I feel like I learn something new every time I read it.

My interest in contractualism and future generations was sparked in 2006 when I was an MSc student of Philip Cook and Paul Kelly at the London School of Economics. They introduced me to Scanlon's contractualism and the non-identity problem, respectively, and for that I am both grateful and aggrieved (again, respectively).

Early on, Cécile Fabre encouraged me to pursue my interest in combining the topics of intergenerational justice and contractualism, of which this book is the culmination, and I am grateful to her for that encouragement. I would also like to thank Cécile, Nadia Khalaf, Margaret Moore, Simon Caney, David Miller, and Gustaf Arrhenius for mentorship and encouragement to start and continue a career in political philosophy.

Conversations with many people in the years since have influenced my thinking on these topics, particularly with Caleb Althorpe, Gustaf Arrhenius, SJ Beard, Paul Billingham, Daniel Butt, Krister Bykvist, Tim Campbell, Simon Caney, Owen Clifton, Göran Duus-Otterström, Stephen Gardiner, Clare Heyward, Christine Hobden, Don Hubin, Robert Huseby, Charles Jones, Corey Katz, Niko Kolodny, Karin Kuhlemann, Rahul Kumar, Erik Magnusson, Kritika Maheshwari, Dan McDermott, Susan McNair, Tim Meijers, David Miller, Julia Mosquera, Tim Mulgan, Serena Olsaretti, Martin O'Neill, Felix Pinkert, Katharina Berndt

Rasmussen, Melinda Roberts, Dominic Roser, Anthony Skelton, H. Orri Stefánsson, Stephen Sweet, Émile P. Torres, Richard Vernon, Jeremy Waldron, Natalie Weigum, Rivka Weinberg, and Caleb Yong.

For insightful comments and questions that improved several chapters, I'd like to thank audiences at the Institute for Futures Studies in Stockholm, the Nuffield College Workshop in Political Theory, the Braga Meetings on Ethics and Political Philosophy, the Pavia Graduate Conference in Philosophy, the MANCEPT Workshops in Political Theory, the University of Pompeu Fabra, and Steve Gardiner's fantastic upper-year ethics seminar students at the University of Washington. Many thanks are also due to Caleb Althorpe, Jake Collie, and Mariana Matias for very helpful research assistance along the way.

Next, I want to thank my editor, Peter Ohlin, and the anonymous reviewers for Oxford University Press for encouragement and comments that significantly improved the book. Thanks also to Daniel Butt, Charles Jones, Martin O'Neill, and Richard Vernon for very helpful comments on previous drafts. My greatest intellectual debt in this project is to Simon Caney, who has always been so generous with his time. I thank him for his guidance, detailed notes, and conversations about earlier versions of the manuscript in his incredible book-lined room at Magdalen College, Oxford. He should not be held responsible for any split infinitives that survived his cull. Any other errors I blame on my cat, Smokey, who regularly walked on my keyboard throughout the writing process.

I must also acknowledge the generous financial assistance of several different bodies, including the Institute for Futures Studies' Climate Ethics and Future Generations project funded by Riksbankens Jubileumsfond, the Swedish Research Council, the Social Sciences and Humanities Research Council of Canada, Lincoln College, Oxford, the Sloane-Robinson Foundation, the Oxford Department of Politics & International Relations, the Society for Applied Philosophy, and the University of Warwick.

The Political Science Department at the University of Western Ontario has been my academic home since 2019 and has generously supplied me with excellent research assistance and funding.

The book draws on work that was previously published in the *Canadian Journal of Philosophy*, *Social Theory and Practice*, and *Ethical Theory and Moral Practice*. I am grateful to the anonymous reviewers for their comments on these papers, and to the publishers of those journals for permission to reuse some of that material here.

Finally, I would like to thank my family and friends, who supported me throughout the writing process, some (my son, Christopher) by distracting me from my work, and others (my mother, Penny) for helping to distract the distraction so that I could actually finish it.

This book is dedicated to my late grandmother, Rhoda Finneron, who would have been very proud, but bemused at the subject since, as she put it once, well before I was interested in this topic: "The world is going to hell in a handbasket anyway, so what's the point worrying about how bad the basket will be?"

A 'Mind-Bending Topic'

John Rawls once wrote that intergenerational ethics "subjects any ethical theory to severe if not impossible tests," and Brian Barry described it as a "mind-bending topic."[1] One reason it is so challenging is that there are a number of striking differences between intra- and intergenerational relations that give us reason to question the extent to which we can use the same principles or methods from the *intra*generational context in the *inter*generational context. But despite its complexities, Rawls, Barry, and most other philosophers agree that the topic is crucially important.

Intergenerational ethics is not just philosophically interesting; it is also of great *practical* importance, especially given human beings' ability to affect the quality of life of the people who will inhabit the world in the future. Recent discussion has tended to centre on climate change, but other policies will also have significant consequences for the future. For example, we continue to use up non-renewable resources at a high rate, the world's population has been growing steadily, and there has been a general loss of biodiversity over the years.[2] These factors will affect the quantity and quality of resources available for future people to use, the quality of life these people will have, and the sort of natural environment they are able to enjoy.

---

[1] John Rawls (1999), *A Theory of Justice*, rev. ed. (Belknap Press of Harvard University Press): 251; Brian Barry (1991), *Essays in Political Theory: Liberty and Justice*, vol. 2 (Clarendon Press).

[2] Nevada Colorado River Commission (2002), "World Fossil Fuel Reserves and Projected Depletion"; United Nations, Department of Economic and Social Affairs (2004), "Population to 2300"; Secretariat of the Convention on Biological Diversity (2010), "Third Global Biodiversity Outlook".

It is not just environmental factors that are of concern. As I write this in early 2023, we are in the twilight (hopefully) of the COVID-19 pandemic. Governments around the world have poured trillions of dollars into fighting the economic and health effects of the pandemic and this money will eventually have to be paid back, in all likelihood primarily by people who have not even been born yet. It is crucial to understand what it is we owe to future people in terms of both providing benefits (e.g., a good environment) and preventing burdens (e.g., large public debts).

The first task is to delineate the parameters of the question. Although the term 'intergenerational ethics' might properly include all generations past, present, and future, for my purposes I will be considering only the relationship between current and future people, and not the question of what one generation might owe to its predecessors. When I refer to 'future people' or, interchangeably, to 'future generations', I will be referring to people who do not yet exist rather than to those who are very young and yet to become adults. The future people I have in mind include those who will be born in twenty years and therefore whose lives will overlap with ours at least for a time, but also remote future generations with whom our lives will never overlap. However, I will primarily have in mind—and likely refer explicitly to—these remote, non-overlapping future generations, as they are the 'harder case' for reasons I will discuss shortly.

The seemingly simple question 'What do we owe to future people?' actually contains a number of different questions, including what principle(s) of justice, if any, apply over time, and to whom. But it also extends beyond considerations of justice to include other moral ideals such as basic humanitarian duties and the value of promoting good states of affairs that are not necessarily considered to be matters of 'justice'. For example, it might be thought that it would be bad if humans became extinct, but it could not be said to be *unjust* since there is no one to whom or for whom it is unjust or unfair.[3] So we may believe that we ought not to choose principles that result in the end of the human species, but the objection to such principles would not arise from a claim about injustice.

Scope and Content

Work on intergenerational ethics typically divides into two strands. The first type of work addresses what I call the 'scope question' and queries whether morality and/or justice's scope includes future people.[4] A positive answer to the scope question suggests that future people ought to be included as objects of—not necessarily equal—moral concern and vice versa. For those who find that future people *are* included in the scope of morality, a further question arises: does morality's reach extend to possible people or is it limited only to actual future people?[5]

The second strand assumes (or has determined) that we have obligations to future generations and focuses on filling in the *content* of such obligations; this I call the 'content question'.[6] One part of the content question is *currency*. What kinds of things are to be distributed amongst current and future people? Options could

---

[3] For more examples, see John Broome (2004), *Weighing Lives* (Oxford University Press).

[4] Examples of those answering the justification/scope question include Axel Gosseries (2009), "Three Models of Intergenerational Reciprocity," in *Intergenerational Justice*, ed. Axel Gosseries and Lukas Meyer (Oxford University Press); Avner De-Shalit (1995), *Why Posterity Matters: Environmental Policies and Future Generations* (Routledge).

[5] Because our actions affect who in particular is born, there are two types of future people. *Actual* people are those who will certainly exist at some point in the future; *possible* people are the much larger group whose existence is contingent on our choices and who may never exist.

[6] Examples include Edward Page (2007), "Justice Between Generations: Investigating a Sufficientarian Approach," *Journal of Global Ethics* 3(1) and Brian Barry (1991), "The Ethics of Resource Depletion," in *Essays in Political Theory: Liberty and Justice* (Clarendon Press).

include opportunities for welfare or capabilities, money, social and political institutions, natural resources and other primary goods, or even life itself if one considers existence to be something that can be distributed to people. Once we have decided *what* to distribute, we need to know *how* to distribute it. According to what principle(s) should we distribute the right things to the right people? This is where theories like utilitarianism, sufficientarianism, and egalitarianism (to name a few examples) come in. They are theories that tell us how to distribute the things we have deemed appropriate (currency) to the people we decided were owed them (those included in the scope).

A comprehensive theory of intergenerational ethics will justify including future people in the scope of morality (answering the scope problem) and tell us the currency and pattern of what we owe them (answering the content problem). One approach to finding such a theory could be to add future people and stir: take your preferred theory among contemporaries and simply apply it to future people. Whatever we owe to contemporaries, we also owe to future people for the same reasons and in the same way. For example, if we are Rawlsians, then we might include future people under the veil of ignorance; if we are utilitarians, we might seek to maximize utility across all generations, and so on. This approach regards the treatment of future people as if it were no different from that of contemporaries. The potential problem with this approach is that there are a number of ways in which the situation of future people *is* quite different, and so one might reasonably wonder whether we really can just apply the theories we use *intra*generationally to the *inter*generational context.

Challenges for the Scope Problem

There are a number of reasons that including future people in the scope of morality is not necessarily straightforward. The most obvious of these is that the people to whom we are trying to determine what we owe do not exist. This simple fact raises a whole host of complications, particularly for theories that depend on reciprocity, (relative) equality of power, or affective ties to ground obligations to others.

Since we do not interact with remote future generations, we cannot straightforwardly cooperate with them for mutual advantage. Relatedly, there is an unequal power relationship between current and future people. Current people have the ability to affect future people's quality of life and desires, but remote future people do not have the same ability to affect ours, at least not while we are still alive. But even if we accepted the claim that future people could later harm us through frustrating our posthumous interests or reputations,[7] there is still an asymmetric, unequal power relationship since future people are not able to affect the quality of our lives as we live them now, whereas we can affect the quality of life that future people actually live. This is a problem for ethical theories that are based on mutual advantage or reciprocity and rely on the parties having basically equal circumstances. Finally, there is an absence of strong affective ties between the current generation and remote future generations, which challenges theories that are based on a sense of community or affection. We will likely feel a sense of affection towards our very close descendants, but this feeling wanes considerably as the generations grow more distant.

These factors make identifying, explaining, and justifying moral obligations to future people more challenging than simply choosing whatever our preferred intragenerational theory is and assuming it applies equally well to future generations. An essential first step is to ensure that one's preferred theory can be grounded despite a lack of reciprocity, equality, or affective ties. It must also show where the motivation to act morally to future people comes from if we will

---

[7] See Barbara Baum Levenbook (1984), "Harming Someone After His Death," *Ethics* 94(3); John O'Neill (1993), "Future Generations: Present Harms," *Philosophy* 68(263).

never know them or interact with them, or when we have little or nothing to gain materially from them.

In addition to these more general issues, two problems in what is known as 'population ethics' also pose a challenge for the scope question: the non-identity problem and the question of optimal population size. These problems matter because they are the focus of intensive debate among population ethicists, and a theory succumbing to one of these challenges is thought by some to be a decisive argument against its overall success as a theory of intergenerational ethics.

The Non-Identity Problem

The non-identity problem challenges the justification problem by questioning the claim that our actions can harm future people. The identity of a particular person depends, at least in part, on their genetic and biological makeup.[8] The genetic component of a person's identity comes from the exact pair of gametes that were joined together at conception. This combination obviously depends on who the parents are because, as Parfit, slightly tongue-in-cheek, put it, the answer to the question 'Who would I be if my parents had married other people?' is obviously 'no one.'[9] Quite simply, if your mother had conceived with a man other than your father, *you* would not exist. *Someone* would exist, but they would not be you.

It is not just the identities of the parents that are relevant but also *when* these two people conceive, because their timing affects which specific egg and sperm combination conceives the child. This is known as the Time-Dependence Claim: "if any particular person had not been conceived within a month of the time when he was

---

[8] There is a branch of thought that sees genetics as largely irrelevant to personal identity. I will not discuss this here, but for a discussion of some of these positions and a response, see Derek Parfit (1984), *Reasons and Persons* (Clarendon Press): 351–55.
[9] Ibid., 351.

in fact conceived, he would in fact never have existed."[10] The Time-Dependence Claim trades on the fact that a woman releases a different egg each month and so an embryo conceived in June would spring from a different egg than an embryo conceived in July. The resulting child's genetic identity will vary depending on whether they were conceived in June or July.

Because of the Time-Dependence Claim, many decisions we make now will affect the identities of future people. Some decisions, like consciously choosing when to have a child, are obvious; others, like going out for a walk, are not.[11] The fact that what we do affects who is conceived leads to the famous non-identity problem. The problem, stated succinctly:

> *Non-Identity Problem:* If an action we perform causes a person to exist with a very bad but still barely-worth-living life, our action has not harmed him since if we had not performed it, he would never have existed.

The problem can be illustrated through two contrasting examples. First, imagine Christopher and Diana conceive a child, Ernest. Six months into Diana's pregnancy the couple finds themselves in financial difficulties. They meet a wealthy man who offers them $100,000 to buy Ernest and keep him as a slave. They sign an enforceable contract to that effect and when Ernest is born, they dutifully sell him to the man who uses him as a slave and causes him to suffer in various ways but still live a barely-worth-living life.[12] This is known as a *same people choice* because Ernest would be born regardless of whether or not his parents accept the man's offer.

---

[10] Ibid., 352.
[11] To see why this is so, suppose that on your walk you meet your future life partner and later conceive a child with this person. If you had not gone for the walk, you would not have met your mate and the child that later resulted would never have existed.
[12] This example and the next are modifications of Kavka's in Gregory Kavka (1982), "The Paradox of Future Individuals," *Philosophy & Public Affairs* 11(2): 100.

Because Ernest was already conceived before the harmful act (selling him into slavery) was performed, the non-identity problem does not present a challenge to the claim that he is made worse off by his parents' decision since he would have existed either way. Assuming Christopher and Diana would have given him a better life if they had raised him themselves, Ernest is clearly made worse off by their choice to sell him into slavery.[13]

In the second example, Christopher and Diana run into their financial difficulties and sign the enforceable contract with the wealthy man *before* conceiving a child, Frank, to be his slave. If they had not signed the contract, they would still have had a child (Greta) but at a different time, later, once they were back on their feet. The child they in fact have (Frank) owes his existence to the agreement; if it were not for the contract, he never would have existed. This is a *different people choice* because the identity of the child who is born is contingent on the decision they made. In this case the non-identity problem does challenge the claim that Frank is made worse off by his parents' decision because the alternative is that he never would have existed—Greta would have instead. Since *ex hypothesi* Frank nevertheless has a life worth living, his parents have not made him worse off or harmed him by conceiving him and subsequently selling him to be a slave. The challenge of the non-identity problem is to explain why Christopher and Diana's decision was wrong despite the fact that Frank was not harmed by it.

We need not be making a decision about whether or not to have a child for the non-identity problem to rear its ugly head because completely random and seemingly unrelated actions also affect who in particular is born. As such, they result in scenarios where, although those who are born have disadvantages of some kind, they cannot be said to have been made worse off than they otherwise would have been. For example, imagine we develop a weapon that, when activated, not only kills people in the vicinity but also

---

[13] Perhaps an unwarranted assumption given their child-selling ways!

causes genetic mutations in the survivors. These mutations are then passed on to the children they later conceive and result in physical and developmental disabilities, illnesses, etc. These disabilities will be directly attributable to the weapon's use, but so will be the children's existences. For if the weapon had not been used, people would not have fled the area, needed time to recuperate, and so on. These actions all affect when and with whom the survivors procreate and therefore also the identities of the people who will be born with disabilities. The non-identity problem suggests that if a child born with such defects later has at least a minimally decent life, he cannot claim that the weapon made him worse off since if it were not for the weapon, he in particular would not exist.

The fact that the child has a life that is (even barely) worth living is relevant in explaining why the action did not make him worse off. All things considered, if it is the case that his life is not even worth living due to the genetic defects, one could consider that his life was worse than no life at all. On the contrary, if he nevertheless deems his life to be worth living despite his disabilities, it cannot be said that causing him to exist harmed him because, all things considered, his life contains more benefits than burdens and he is better off than if he had not been born at all. One could argue that even if his life is worth living, he has been made worse off in just one area of his life. However, the Time-Dependence Claim disputes this, since *he* could not ever have been better off. *He* in particular could not exist without genetic deformities, and the disability and his existence are inextricably linked.

The non-identity problem is a challenge to accounts of obligations to the future because it suggests that we cannot harm people in the future unless it is the case that the people who are created will exist regardless of what actions we take. Since such surety is generally possible only in very specific circumstances, the implication is that in many cases the actions we perform cannot harm future people because they will not make these people worse off, even if they have lives that are only barely worth living. If no one is harmed, the challenge is to explain why we should care about the negative effects our actions have on people in the future.

The problem makes several assumptions:

(i) An action (A) harms a person (P) when they are made worse off by it relative to either a temporal or counterfactual baseline.
(ii) If P has a life barely worth living and would not exist if it were not for A, he is not made worse off and is not harmed by A.
(iii) A is not wrong if P is not harmed as a result.
Therefore:
(iv) Action A, which causes P to exist with a life just barely worth living, is not wrong.
But:
(v) There is an intuitive moral objection to actions that cause people to have only barely-worth-living lives, especially when the burdens in question were avoidable.

The fifth point, (v), is the key to understanding why the non-identity problem is a 'problem' and not just an interesting philosophical quirk. If we did not share the intuition in (v) we would have no objection to accepting (iv). The conclusion that our negligent actions are not wrong because they do not make future people worse off is a problem only if we share the intuition that there is something nonetheless wrong with such actions. There are some who are willing to bite the bullet and accept that seemingly wrong acts are in fact permissible,[14] but I think most of us probably believe that we should care about the quality of life of the people we create and consequently look for ways 'around' the non-identity problem.

There are many different replies offered by philosophers which generally challenge one of the premises upon which the problem

---

[14] David Heyd (1992), *Genethics: Moral Issues in the Creation of People* (University of California Press).

rests.[15] However, there has been no universally accepted solution and it remains an issue that political theorists and philosophers tackling the question of intergenerational obligations must address.

Optimal Population Size

The second puzzle in population ethics that affects the scope and content problems is that of optimal population size. We can affect the size of future generations both directly, by selecting specific reproductive policies, and indirectly, by selecting policies that ultimately affect the number of children people choose to have.[16] The population size in turn can positively or negatively affect the quality of life that future people will have. Too large a population may mean a low quality of life due to housing shortages, overcrowded schools, and a high demand for natural resources, whilst too small a population may not be able to continue the human species or support the robust economy that is required to maintain public services. How to determine the ideal population size raises some hard questions and cannot be dealt with easily.

According to one theory of value—total utilitarianism—provided that the people who exist have lives that are worth living, the larger the population, the better. This is because each worth-living life adds to the total value of well-being that exists in the world: the more lives that are lived, even if they are just barely worth living, the higher the level of total well-being. This leads to what Parfit called the 'repugnant conclusion':

---

[15] Elizabeth Harman (2004), "Can We Harm and Benefit in Creating?," *Philosophical Perspectives* 18(1); James Woodward (1986), "The Non-Identity Problem," *Ethics* 96(4): 811–18; Parfit, *Reasons and Persons*: 364–65.

[16] For example, if we select a policy of resource conservation, this may mean that people choose to have fewer children since they are required to save more for the future and may not be able to afford more children.

Repugnant Conclusion: For any possible large population, all with a very high quality of life, there must be some much larger imaginable population whose existence, if other things are equal, would be better, even though its members have lives that are barely worth living.[17]

He asks us to imagine two possible worlds. In world A there are 1 billion people with very high qualities of life. In world Z there are 10 billion people with lives that are just barely worth living. Since any life that is worth living, however wretched, increases the total amount of well-being, world Z actually contains more well-being than world A. Therefore, we should prefer world Z. In short, total utilitarianism allows a loss in an individual's well-being to be outweighed by a sufficient increase in the number of people living, and if we believe that world Z is worse than world A, we have a strong case for rejecting total utilitarianism. However, it is not just total utilitarianism which leads to the conclusion that a very large population of people with barely-worth-living lives is better than a smaller population of people with excellent lives.[18] Although there are those who believe that the repugnant conclusion only appears repugnant because of our own assumptions and biases,[19] I am inclined to reject these views and agree with Tim Mulgan that the intuition is so consistent "with a general picture of morality we must adopt if we are . . . to practise moral philosophy at all" that it must be taken seriously.[20] For that reason, it is

---

[17] Parfit, *Reasons and Persons:* 388.

[18] Although I do not discuss them here, other positions that have been accused of leading to the repugnant conclusion are discussed in Nils Holtug (2007), "On Giving Priority to Possible Future People," in *Hommage à Wlodek: Philosophical Papers Dedicated to Wlodek Rabinowicz,* ed. T. Rønnow-Rasmussen et al. (Lund University); Nils Holtug (2010), *Persons, Interests, and Justice* (Oxford University Press); Tim Mulgan (2006), *Future People: A Moderate Consequentialist Account of Our Obligations to Future Generations* (Clarendon Press); Parfit, *Reasons and Persons.*

[19] For example, Jesper Ryberg (1996), "Is the Repugnant Conclusion Repugnant?," *Philosophical Papers* 25 and Torbjörn Tännsjö (2002), "Why We Ought to Accept the Repugnant Conclusion," *Utilitas* 14(3).

[20] Mulgan, *Future People:* 60.

desirable that a theory of intergenerational obligations not imply the repugnant conclusion.

Significantly less discussed is the opposite problem that also concerns population size: human extinction. Some theories may (inadvertently or otherwise) permit or even promote a population size of zero, meaning the extinction of the human species. For example, negative utilitarianism holds that rather than trying to maximize happiness, we ought to minimize suffering. Unfortunately, since virtually every human life will contain at least a small degree of unhappiness, suffering is minimized when no lives are lived at all.[21]

However, there may be good reasons to prefer that human life continues, perhaps due to some intrinsic value of humans themselves, or for person-affecting reasons. Because the topic of human extinction is so underexplored by philosophers (compared to, for example, the repugnant conclusion), it is hard to say for certain whether philosophers think that endorsing or even permitting extinction disqualifies a theory of intergenerational ethics. I suspect it is likely that they would, but in Chapter 5 I will be trying to convince you that they should not (always).

What I Will and Won't Do

My aims in this book are twofold. The first is to justify a distinctive set of answers to the scope and content questions—specifically, why we have obligations to which future people, and what the content of those obligations is. My central claim is that contractualism is a comprehensive theory of intergenerational ethics because it can answer the scope question without falling afoul of the special problems mentioned earlier (non-identity problem, etc.) and the

---

[21] See, for example, David Benatar (2006), *Better Never to Have Been: The Harm of Coming into Existence* (Clarendon Press).

content question because it elicits what I take to be plausible ethical principles governing our actions towards future generations. That it does this supports my second aim, which is to provide additional support for contractualism as a moral philosophy in general by showing its ability to accommodate future people and generate plausible principles of intergenerational obligations.

Here is how I will do it. Chapter 1 outlines two competing versions of contractualism (Rawls' and Scanlon's) and defends the use of the latter over the former. Next, in Chapter 2, I show how Scanlon's contractualism answers the justification problem, including a response to the non-identity problem. Chapter 3 introduces the concept of 'reason-balanced sufficientarianism' upon which my arguments in the remaining substantive chapters depend. Chapters 3–5 develop principles of intergenerational justice regarding natural resources, procreation, and population size respectively. While Chapters 4 and 5 *can* stand alone, they will be better understood (and more persuasive) if the reader has read Chapter 3. In Chapter 6 I consider what principles apply in situations of uncertainty—when we do not know what future people will need, or how our actions will impact them. Chapter 7 takes the principles developed and tackles real-world individual and policy choices, directly answering the titular question 'What do we owe to future people?'

What this book will not do is respond to specific criticisms that have been levied at contractualism. For one thing, many others have written extensive defences of it against its critics, and I would simply be reinventing the wheel to reproduce their arguments here. Instead, I aim my thoughts at those who already find contractualism convincing, or at least initially plausible and who want to know more about its account of intergenerational ethics. Those who are on the fence should find the coherence and plausibility of the contractualist account of intergenerational ethics developed here sufficient to be convinced of the superiority of the contractualist approach in general, especially given the inadequacy of some other ways of approaching this issue.

1
Contractualism(s)

What About Rawls?

This book develops a contractualist account of our ethical obligations to future people, but when I have presented the ideas in this book at various conferences or workshops, the most common first question I get is 'Why not Rawls?' so I will dutifully answer it here before delving into 'Why Scanlon?'

Scanlon and Rawls share the belief that political and moral norms are determined by what can be justified to each person, consistent with a fundamental respect for the rational moral agency of others. The wish to justify one's actions to others is based on an intrinsic desire rather than some strategic or instrumental aim. Scanlon and Rawls have this claim in common, but they differ in important ways such as the nature of the contract they use and the knowledge and motivations of the parties involved in the agreement. Whereas Scanlon asks what others could reasonably reject, Rawls seeks the set of principles that everybody would *accept* under the conditions of the veil of ignorance and general mutual disinterest.

My short answer to the 'What about Rawls?' question is that his version of contractualism cannot answer the scope question without logical contradictions or inconsistencies with the rest of his theory of justice. My point here is not just to explain why we should not accept this rival contractualist account of intergenerational justice, but also to identify potential stumbling blocks my preferred Scanlonian version of contractualism could encounter. Given that they are part of the same tradition, what do we learn from what goes wrong with Rawls' version that Scanlon's can help us with?

The Argument for the Just Savings Principle

Rawls' treatment of intergenerational justice is tantalisingly concise, taking up only nine of the almost six hundred pages in *A Theory of Justice*.[1] Nonetheless, they pack quite a punch, and there is a lot to unearth in those nine pages.

The aim of Rawls' contract is a just society in which just institutions and basic liberties are secured for all, including future people. Because each generation has a natural duty to share in the burden of securing the institutions required to realise and preserve such a society in a long-term scheme of cooperation, once the parties in the original position have selected the two principles of justice for contemporaries, they are asked to choose a principle of savings for the future. The conditions of the original position are basically unchanged (I will discuss this in more detail later) and the parties are concerned with ensuring that whenever they live, their society is just.

To determine who is party to the contract, Rawls initially takes what he calls the 'present time of entry' interpretation (PTE). The PTE consists of two assumptions, one explicit and one strongly implied. First, the explicit—the parties know that they are all contemporaries and members of the same generation: "Those in the original position know, then, that they are contemporaries."[2] Second, they also know that they shall be the first generation subject to the savings principle they choose. Although he never says so explicitly, this second part of the PTE is implied from the number of times Rawls refers to the just savings principle taking effect with the generation in the original position. Consider for example, the following comments:

---

[1] John Rawls (1971), *A Theory of Justice* (Belknap Press of Harvard University Press).
[2] Ibid., 292.

(1) "they can favor their generation by refusing to make any sacrifices at all for their successors."[3]
(2) "obviously if all generations are to gain [from the savings principle] (except perhaps the first)..."[4]
(3) "there is no reason for them to agree to undertake any saving whatever.... Either earlier generations have saved or they have not."[5]

The only way for the parties to 'favor their generation by refusing to make any sacrifices' (1) is if they know that the just savings principle begins with them. If they were not the first generation, this would mean that the parties would suffer some loss by adopting a rule that refuses to make sacrifices for successive generations since their predecessors' following such a principle would make them worse off. Rawls must be assuming that the generation in the original position would not lose from such a principle but would actually benefit from it. The only generation of which this could be true is the first. In (2) he says that the first generation will not benefit from the savings principle. Then in passage (3) he argues that there is no reason for the parties to save since they will not benefit from savings. Putting (2) and (3) together, it is clear that Rawls intended the parties to be the first generation subject to the principle. Adding that 'either earlier generations have saved or they have not' means that there is nothing the parties can do to affect what they inherit, and this lends more weight to the claim that the savings principle under scrutiny will begin with their generation and not earlier ones.

The veil of ignorance also deprives the parties of the knowledge of the generation of which they are a part and the state of civilization of their society. They have no idea whether their generation

---

[3] Ibid., 140.
[4] Ibid., 291.
[5] Ibid., 292.

will turn out to be poor or wealthy, agricultural or industrious, and so on. The purpose of this is to maintain impartiality in decision-making and to ensure that the parties will "choose principles the consequences of which they are prepared to live with whatever generation they turn out to belong to."[6] Rawls believes that the two provisos in the PTE and the veil of ignorance together ensure that all generations are virtually represented in the original position. It is unclear why Rawls insists that the parties must all be members of the *same* generation, but I will say more about this later.

It is to resolve the problem of the first generation that Rawls changes his usual assumption of the parties as self-interested and mutually disinterested, and adopts the peculiar assumption that they are heads of households and care for their descendants.[7] The parties are now regarded as representing family lines with ties of sentiment between successive generations. Each party would be concerned only about the next one or two generations, but since those people would then be concerned about the next two, this creates an overlapping chain to the distant future, with each future person having a previous person who is concerned about them. Rawls believes this explains why the parties in the original position would choose to save even though they do not benefit from this choice.

Rawls claims that in these conditions the parties would not choose a principle that required generations to save extensively in order to make later generations as wealthy as possible. Rather, he argued that to maximise their chances of living in a just society, it is rational for the parties to choose a principle that simply ensures that the basic institutions of society are just. To this end, during the 'accumulation phase' generations must do their part to save resources to pass on more to the next generation than they themselves received, in order to assist the later generation in securing

---

[6] Ibid., 137.
[7] Ibid., 288–92.

basic liberties and just institutions. Once these institutions are firmly in place and not in danger of disappearing, the required net accumulation falls to zero and generations are no longer required to save—Rawls calls this the 'steady state phase'.[8] Once the steady state is reached, generations may, of course, choose to save if they wish, but if they do, it is for reasons other than duties of justice.

Rawls is keen to emphasize that the steady state phase is not necessarily a time of great abundance. While there is, of course, a connection between a minimum degree of material wealth and the ability to realize fully just institutions, "it is a mistake to believe that a just and good society must wait upon a high material standard of life."[9] Indeed, he wants to dispel the very notion that generations should save simply in order to make later generations wealthier. He thinks that, assuming that economic growth remains constant or increases, this would require earlier (poorer) generations to save for the benefit of later (wealthier) ones. Such a thought would be inconsistent with the spirit of the rest of Rawls' theory of justice, which gives priority to the worst-off because requiring the poorer, earlier generations to save would actually be giving priority to the best-off. Rawls recognizes this, and while he does not want to require generations to save for simply economic reasons, he is also uncomfortable with the conclusion that generations are not required to save at all. In fact, he rejects an intergenerational difference principle in part because it would sanction zero savings: "It is now clear why the difference principle does not apply to the savings problem. There is no way for later generations to improve the situation of the least fortunate first generation. The principle is inapplicable and would seem to imply, if anything, that there be no saving at all. Thus, the problem of saving must be treated in another fashion."[10]

---

[8] Ibid., 287.
[9] Ibid., 290.
[10] Ibid., 291.

Who Is in the Original Position and What Do They Know?

Since Rawls derives the just savings principle from what he claims the parties in the original position would choose, it is crucial to examine who the parties in the original position are and what they know. I will consider three options open to Rawls, two of which he considered himself and a third that he did not discuss. The table below shows the membership configuration and knowledge of the parties in each of the three options I will consider.

Formulation	Members of the Original Position	What They Know	What They Do Not Know
(i) **Rawls' Original Formulation** (PTE)	Members of one generation	They are all contemporaries They are all members of the first generation	Practical facts about their generation—industriousness, wealth, etc.
(ii) **Rawls' Revised Formulation** (**Atemporal Interpretation**)	Members of one generation *or* Members of many generations	They will exist at some point	Practical facts about themselves/their generation When they/their generation will exist
(iii) **Alternative Formulation**	Members of many generations	Nothing	Practical facts about their generation When their generation will exist (if at all) If they will come to exist or not

Rawls' Original Formulation

Let's start with formulation (i), which is the route Rawls originally followed in *A Theory of Justice*. He believes that it is important for the parties to be contemporaries and to maintain the 'present time of entry' interpretation. Recall that one assumption of the PTE is that the principles the parties choose will be effective only from the present onwards into the future (i.e., they can have no effect on the past). But Rawls thinks this fact would dissuade the parties from adopting any savings plan at all. This is because, although they do not know to which generation they all belong, they do know that they will be the first generation subject to the savings principle they choose, gaining nothing from it, so they will choose not to save. He writes, for example, that the "parties can favor their generation by refusing to make any sacrifices at all for their successors; they simply acknowledge the principle that no one has a duty to save for posterity."[11]

Given that he believes it has this (rather significant!) pitfall, it is unclear exactly why he insists on maintaining the PTE interpretation. In fact, he seems to take it as an obvious truth without any clear defence. He refers directly to this stipulation twice, both times writing as though it has already been argued for and accepted. The first occasion is when he is describing the conditions of the veil of ignorance (§24) and says, "Since the persons in the original position know that they are contemporaries . . ."[12] The second refers back to the first, and he says, "As we noted earlier (§24), it is best to take the present time of entry interpretation."[13] Indeed, it *was* so noted earlier, but only in passing, and it was never defended. I have been unable to locate any prior defense of this interpretation, and it is almost as if a piece of §24 was accidentally omitted.

---

[11] Ibid., 140.
[12] Ibid., 140.
[13] Ibid., 292.

Moreover, there seem to be good reasons for abandoning the 'present time of entry' interpretation altogether. As Jane English suggests, if he gave it up, he would not need to adjust the motivation assumption in order to solve the problem of the first generation. Suppose that the parties included people from different generations and were not all contemporaries. In these circumstances they could not assume that they were all members of the first generation to follow the savings schedule. Given this, they would not ignore the claims of all generations subsequent to the first. In that case, self-interested individuals would probably choose to equalize resources among generations in case, when the veil was lifted, they turned out to be members of the first generation.[14] As I shall argue in the next section, however, this solution has problems of its own.

But before moving on, we should ask if we *should* preserve the original motivation assumption—namely, that the parties in the original position are mutually disinterested without ties of sentiment towards each other—or whether it is better to follow Rawls and assume that the parties have a concern for their descendants that stretches over at least one or two generations. The first problem with the latter assumption is that it is inconsistent with the spirit of Rawls' aims in writing *A Theory of Justice*. Rawls stipulates that the parties in the original position are self-interested and mutually disinterested.[15] That is, they are rational actors seeking to maximize their personal gain subject to the limitations of the veil of ignorance and have no special relationships with or interest in others. The principles of justice that they agree on are the products of their interest in maximizing their own well-being and having no particular feelings (positive or negative) about each other or how well others do relative to themselves. Rawls does not want his theory to rely upon (what he takes to be) questionable assumptions about human nature, and in §22 he states that the "postulate of mutual

---

[14] Jane English (1977), "Justice Between Generations," *Philosophical Studies* 31(2).
[15] Rawls, *A Theory of Justice*: 128.

disinterest . . . is made to ensure that the principles of justice do not depend upon [such] assumptions."[16] Yet also in §22, when he turns to discussing intergenerational justice, it is stipulated that they care for at least one or two future generations. The parties care about the welfare of their immediate descendants, so every person in the original position cares about somebody and every person in the generation that follows has somebody who cares about them.[17] But why are the parties not able to have concern for other people when dealing with contemporaries but are able to carry such a concern for others when considering intergenerational justice? Rawls never explains why it is appropriate for the parties to feel altruistic towards the next generation but not towards members of their own generation, nation, culture, or so on.

Furthermore, the altered motivation assumption seems to be an ad hoc solution to a seemingly unpalatable result of the original position and veil of ignorance as Rawls originally constructed it. Stipulating that the parties ought to consider themselves to be representing family lines or households may be biased against those who turn out not to have children. Ernest Partridge goes so far as to argue that this violates two constraints (generality and universality) of the concept of right. Since these constraints are supposed to mean that "no one is able to formulate principles especially designed to advance his own cause,"[18] Partridge argues that the 'cause' of being a head of family is a particular interest in conflict with the interests of those who decide to remain childless.[19]

Don Hubin suggests that this problem of bias may be sidestepped somewhat by arguing that the parties do not know that they *do* have descendants that they care about, merely that they *may*. They know that when the veil is lifted, they may turn out to have their

---

[16] Ibid., 129.
[17] Ibid., 128.
[18] Ibid., 140.
[19] Ernest Partridge (1976), "Rawls and the Duty to Posterity," PhD thesis, University of Utah: 188.

own interests bound up in the interests of their descendants, and therefore not be purely egoistic. For this reason, they will want to minimise the risk that these descendants will be badly off, and will choose to save, even if it does not benefit them (the parties in the original position).[20] However, this solution is still ad hoc. Why stipulate that the parties may find that they care for their descendants, but not their contemporaries in the original position? It is true that the parties are not completely asocial within one generation and may care a little about third parties who are not in the original position. However, saying that the parties *may* care about others is not the same as explicitly stipulating that they want to improve their welfare because their own interests are bound up in others'. They have a choice about whether they want to or not. Intergenerationally, however, Rawls is claiming that the parties *must* be interested in doing well for others—namely, the members of the next one or two generations. In order for this stipulation not to be ad hoc, he needs to provide a reason for it that is not question-begging.

Furthermore, he does not properly justify why it is acceptable to alter the motivation assumption to accommodate his intuition about the need for intergenerational savings, but not to change it if we disagree with the principles the parties in the original position choose for justice among contemporaries. If, say, our considered judgement was that full equality of contemporaries was preferable, why could we not alter the motivational assumption to say that all people care about how well their fellows fare?

To sum up the discussion thus far, Rawls has a problem if he makes two simultaneous assumptions:

(1) The parties are contemporaries and know they are the first generation subject to the savings principle.
(2) The parties are mutually disinterested.

---

[20] D. Clayton Hubin (1976), "Justice and Future Generations" *Philosophy & Public Affairs* 6(1): 76–77.

Rawls believes that the combination of (1) and (2) would not give the parties in the original position any reason to save for future generations. Although he does not say so explicitly, it seems that Rawls was unhappy with that result since he looked for a way to avoid it, namely by revising (2) to:

(2*) Parties care for their immediate descendants.

However, (2*) is problematic and ad hoc. No reason is given for changing (2) rather than (1), and (2*) is inconsistent with the rest of his theory of justice.

However, neither (2) nor (2*) explains the source of an obligation to refrain from actions that would not hurt the very next generations, but whose consequences will not be felt until several generations down the line (what Brian Barry called 'sleepers').[21] For example, the effects of resource depletion will not seriously affect our nearest descendants as long as there is still enough for them to survive. It will, however, seriously affect the people who are born when all the resources have disappeared. If the source of motivation for the parties in the original position is a concern for their immediate descendants, what is stopping them from making decisions that will negatively affect not these people but rather those who live three, four, or five generations later, when the original parties' concern has waned? This is particularly true when one considers the connection between the capital accumulation that Rawls desires generations to save and the source of that accumulation—natural resources. If each generation cares only for the next two generations, it will prioritize capital accumulation for them, even if the resource depletion necessary to generate that capital will severely adversely affect generations much further in the future. These long-term problems are real objects of concern because many major decisions do not have immediate

---

[21] Brian Barry (1991), *Essays in Political Theory: Liberty and Justice*, vol. 2 (Clarendon Press): 242.

or short-term effects and it seems that the original position, as it is described by Rawls, cannot cope with them.

However, even if we assume that the people in the original position do care about their descendants, the entire original position thought experiment is redundant. The parties were placed under the veil of ignorance in order to determine what they would choose if they knew nothing about their personal circumstances. In the PTE the parties are the first generation subject to the savings principle, but if we removed the veil, the parties would presumably already know that they are the first generation to which the savings principle would apply and, since *ex hypothesi* they care for at least their immediate descendants, would choose the same principle as Rawls has them choose under the veil. In this case the veil is failing to disguise crucial pieces of information that are relevant to the determination of a principle of just savings—whether or not you have descendants and care for them, and when you will exist. In Rawls' version as it stands, the parties in the original position know these things, so the veil of ignorance and original position do not seem to add anything.

Since adhering to the PTE interpretation made Rawls adopt an unjustifiable and ad hoc motivational assumption, let us now consider an alternative interpretation of the temporal position of the parties in the original position, one that Rawls himself adopts in his later dealings on the subject.

Rawls 2.0 (the 'Atemporal Interpretation')
The main difference between Rawls' revised formulation (ii) and the original (i) is that in the revised version, the original position is composed of actual people who do not know when in the course of time they will exist, whereas in (i) the parties know not just that they are actual people, but also that they would be the first generation subject to the savings principle. When I read §44 of *A Theory of Justice* for the first time, I interpreted the temporal position of the parties not necessarily as the first generation subject to the savings

principle, but in an atemporal way. By atemporal I mean that I imagined the parties to be deliberating in a 'noumenal atemporal green room',[22] as Richards put it, where they do not know when their generation will end up living. Although this interpretation was not the one originally intended by Rawls, many philosophers agreed that it would be a more sensible and productive way to describe the conditions of the original position.[23] In these conditions the parties *would* choose to save because they do not know which generations are 'past', 'present', or 'future' relative to them—where they personally will end up living along this timeline. Thus, "for any Generation X, to which the parties might belong and during which term they might choose to 'use up resources,' there are prior generations which, through an adoption of the same policy, would diminish the prospects of Generation X."[24] This removes the first-generation problem and means that Rawls would not have to alter the motivation assumption. People will choose to save out of self-interest because they would not want to be part of a generation that came late in a chain of non-saving generations. R. M. Hare preempts the objection that people cannot actually affect the past by maintaining that "any difficulties which attend these modifications to the scene arise from the creakings of the stage machinery and not from the logic of the argument. . . . That the [parties] cannot affect the past is strictly irrelevant."[25] In fact, he thinks that interpreting the original position in any other way also fails to recognise the same formal constraints of the concept of right (in particular generality and universality) that Rawls himself drew attention to in an earlier section of *A Theory of Justice* (§23).[26]

---

[22] David Richards (1971), *A Theory of Reasons for Action* (Oxford University Press): 88.
[23] For example, R. M. Hare (1973), "Rawls' Theory of Justice II," *Philosophical Quarterly* 23(92); English, "Justice Between Generations"; Gregory Kavka (1975), "Rawls on Total and Average Utilitarianism," *Philosophical Studies* 27(4).
[24] Partridge, "Rawls and the Duty to Posterity": 181.
[25] Hare, "Rawls' Theory of Justice II": 244.
[26] Ibid., 243.

Rawls later accepts these points, and in his reformulation in *Justice as Fairness: A Restatement* and *Political Liberalism*, he adjusts the reasoning underpinning the savings principle to argue that the parties, when "determining their behavior toward future generations . . . must behave in a way that they would want previous generations to have behaved."[27] Stephen Gardiner calls this the Constraint Principle (CP) because the parties are forced to internalize the concerns of other generations and balance what they stand to gain and lose from any given principle.[28] For instance, a generation might benefit in one way from a policy that requires extremely high rates of savings since they stand to receive a bounty from previous generations. However, it would also require them to save at a very high rate themselves, and thus pass on a very large proportion of what they had received and/or produced. Gardiner thinks the CP excludes principles of no savings at all since the cost of previous generations saving nothing outweighs the potential benefit a given generation would enjoy from not being required to save themselves. The CP also excludes the other extreme, a principle of total savings. The benefit accrued from the previous generation leaving everything behind would be outweighed by the burden of having to do the same for the next generation. The CP has the benefit of not requiring an adjustment to Rawls' motivational assumption since the parties remain mutually disinterested self-maximizers: it is in *their* interest to choose a principle that requires moderate savings since they will likely benefit from the generation before having saved and it would not be overly demanding to do the same for the generations that follow. If the original position is conceived of in this atemporal way, we can accommodate at least the membership component of the PTE and imagine members of

---

[27] John Rawls (2005), *Political Liberalism* (Columbia University Press): 273–74.
[28] Stephen Gardiner (2009), "A Contract on Future Generations," in *Intergenerational Justice*, ed. Axel Gosseries and Lukas Meyer (Oxford University Press).

the same generation choosing a schedule of savings without the need to introduce an ad hoc motivational assumption.

Nevertheless, it still seems rather arbitrary and possibly unfair to limit membership to those of a single generation since the policies that are chosen will affect all generations and it is reasonable to think that the contract should be *between* generations rather than *within* one generation. Since the consequences of the contract will ultimately be felt by all generations and we are not meant to privilege our own time (§45), it makes sense to include multiple generations in the original position. Limiting membership to a single generation does not seem to add anything, and Hubin believes that by arbitrarily limiting membership in the original position to contemporaries of each other, Rawls provides for the actual representation of contemporaries of each other but only the virtual representation of those who come after them. What Hubin finds particularly interesting is that Rawls believes—apparently without any justification—that it makes no difference whether one's contemporaries are virtually or actually represented, but it is essential that those born after the people who are included in the original position be only virtually represented.[29] In order to avoid any potential unfairness, members of various actual generations in the original position could be represented in the original position.

Although he does not defend the merits of limiting membership in the original position to members of the same generation, Rawls does explain that he is keen to preserve this status because he cannot envision the original position any other way. He thinks that including representatives from various generations would be to "stretch fantasy too far" and would mean that the original position "would cease to be a natural guide to intuition and would lack a clear sense."[30] Rawls is right that it is difficult to imagine a gathering

---

[29] Hubin, "Justice and Future Generations": 72. He cites *A Theory of Justice*: 291–92, as evidence of this view.
[30] Rawls, *A Theory of Justice*: 129.

of people who will live at various times in history. But it's also hard to imagine a gathering of people who have no knowledge of their own age, sex, or personal conceptions as the good. As he explicitly says towards the end of §4, the original position is an expository device and we are not to assume that it would be practically possible to replicate it.[31] Why would it be so much more difficult to envision the parties in the original position being members of various different generations than it is to envision them as blinded to these other characteristics under the veil of ignorance?

Whether or not the original position includes members of various generations or just one, what remains constant in this interpretation is that the parties are all 'actual people'. Actual people are those who have existed, do exist, or will exist in the future. Their existence and identities are fixed and are not contingent on any particular decisions or policies we could make and, crucially, the parties *know this*. To some this is self-evident. Cécile Fabre thinks it is plain that "if there is one thing of which the parties can be sure in the original position, it is the fact that they themselves exist,"[32] and others believe it makes sense to confine the parties to those who do or will exist (as opposed to all those who could ever exist) because only those who come to exist have interests and those who never exist do not.[33]

One problem with including only actual people is that it raises the spectre of the non-identity problem by begging the question against both the identities of those in the original position and the number of people who will exist.[34] As we know, the existence of a particular person is contingent on a variety of choices made by their predecessors. The decisions made in the 'atemporal green room' of the original position will affect who exists. Against this it could

---

[31] Ibid., 21.
[32] Cécile Fabre (2007), *Justice in a Changing World* (Polity Press): 34.
[33] See, for example, Jeffrey Reiman (2007), "Being Fair to Future People: The Non-Identity Problem in the Original Position," *Philosophy & Public Affairs* 35(1).
[34] Hubin, "Justice and Future Generations": 74.

be objected that the decisions made in the original position will *not* actually affect the real world because the principle the parties choose may not be the principle that was actually acted upon by previous generations. According to this interpretation, the parties choose principle P, which they would have wanted previous generations to have chosen. But P is not necessarily the principle that the previous generations actually acted upon. Therefore, P will not affect the identities of the people in the original position. However, this argument relies on the PTE interpretation since to assume that their identities will not be affected is to assume that the parties will be the first generation subject to the principle and the PTE has already been shown to be unfounded. Since in this revised formulation the parties do not know when they will end up existing, they choose P atemporally and could exist in time *after* P is chosen. The principle they choose will therefore affect the identities of at least some of those in the original position.

The consequence of this fact is that the atemporal model results in the contract being developed between people whose existence is contingent on the principle chosen. An example may help illustrate this point. Imagine the original position contains people from generations A and B who atemporally agree to a just savings principle that requires extremely high rates of savings. In order to comply with the policy, the people in generation A act in certain ways to protect the environment and preserve non-renewable resources. They may choose to travel less, invest in green technology, adhere to a vegetarian diet, and so on. Each one of these lifestyle choices will affect the people they meet and with whom they choose to procreate in ways no one can predict.[35] So the identities of the people who live in generation B are different than they would have been if generation A had followed a different policy. However,

---

[35] For those who doubt that a savings policy could have such an effect, take investments in green energy as an example. A man might meet his wife at their place of work—say the wind energy plant—whereas if there were no such investment, that same man would

including members of generation B in the original position treats their identities as fixed, even though, as we have seen, their very existence should depend on the choices made in the original position. There is something incoherent about the parties choosing principles of justice when their own existence is contingent on the principle chosen. Any principle chosen in this original position applies also to those who will live earlier in time. As a result, the parties may choose principles that result in their own non-existence.

Necessary persons are those who exist no matter what principle or scenario is chosen, whereas contingent persons are those whose existence depends on different courses of action. So to put the problem another way, stipulating that the parties know they will exist, regardless of the principle chosen, treats them as necessary rather than contingent persons, when in fact, since they are selecting principles that will have a great impact on who is born, they are in all likelihood only contingent persons.

Relatedly, whatever principle is chosen, some people will end up existing and others will not. Assuming that existence is a good thing for those who end up having worthwhile lives, certain people will come to enjoy the goods these lives have to offer. But in order to maintain impartiality in the original position, the veil of ignorance must deprive us of the knowledge of whether we will be beneficiaries of a particular principle or not. Assuming that the parties will exist regardless of what principle they choose violates Rawls' requirement of impartiality. To alter Derek Parfit's example slightly, assuming that we shall certainly exist whatever principle is chosen is like choosing a principle that would greatly advantage

---

not have been working at the wind plant and would have been working in the coal mine. He may easily have met a different woman at the coal mine and have different children. It is also worth noting that even if the original position contains only one generation, the same problem remains. A single generation deliberates not knowing when they will exist, and chooses the policy that the generation before them will have to follow. Thus, the generation in the original position's identities will be contingent on the policy they choose.

women while knowing that we shall certainly be women.[36] The whole point of the veil of ignorance is to ensure that we do not know how a principle will affect us. In Parfit's example, if we know that we are women, we will choose principles that benefit women and vice versa. Plugging existence into the analogy, 'if we know that we will exist, we will choose principles that benefit those who exist.' This may seem obviously true, but Parfit thinks that the original position needs to avoid such partiality in principles of all kinds. It could be the case that removing this particular partiality is impossible because existence is a fact about an individual that must be known in the original position. It is not a property that can be hidden and perhaps may be the only particular personal characteristic that is made known to the parties. Nonetheless, David Heyd argues that even if this is so, it begs the question; his conclusion is that this bars the parties from being able to decide on identity-affecting principles in the original position at all.[37]

One potential solution to this problem could be to conceive of the parties as *representatives* of actual people rather than the actual people themselves. In this case, the parties would not be choosing principles that should affect their own existence. Insofar as it is stipulated that the representatives are trustees representing people who will exist (rather than a sample of those who will come to exist), we can skirt the problem of the parties choosing principles that would affect their own identities. But the non-identity problem is not entirely avoided. If the representatives are each told that they are representing a particular person who will come to exist, they are still choosing principles that should affect the identity of the person they are representing, which is still question-begging. To avoid *this*

---

[36] The actual quotation is: "If we assume that we shall certainly exist, whatever principle is chosen, this is like, when choosing a principle that would greatly disadvantage women, that we shall certainly be men." Parfit, *Reasons and Persons*: 392. I have altered it to make the examples more symmetrical.
[37] David Heyd (1992), *Genethics: Moral Issues in the Creation of People* (University of California Press): 71–74.

problem, we must stipulate that the representatives represent not particular people but, rather, *whoever comes to exist*.

The problem is there's reason to believe that Rawls would reject such an arrangement because of the strains of commitment. Rawls says that in the original position "a person is choosing once and for all the standards which are to govern his life prospects."[38] He says that once the veil is lifted the parties must be prepared to live by whatever principles of justice are chosen in the original position. Trustee representatives as described above will, by definition, *not* live under the principles of justice.

Moreover, in this case we would have people who will not exist (the representatives) choosing for those who will. It seems to me that a person might not choose the same principles when they know they will not be affected by them as they would if they knew they would be. For example, a person might be more likely to expose another person to a higher degree of risk than they themselves would be willing to assume. When 'trustee' representatives are doing the choosing in the original position it does not seem fair to say that the principles chosen will necessarily live up to the strains of commitment since no one in the original position will have to live by these principles. One way to avoid the problem of undue risk imposition would be to stipulate that the representatives are wholly responsible and will not impose burdens on the people they represent that the former would not be willing to accept themselves and that the latter could not live up to. If we go this route, however, we seem to be moving more into an 'impartial observer' view. Rawls' description of such an observer sounds quite similar to the wholly responsible trustee I have just outlined: "he assumes a position where his own interests are not at stake."[39] But appealing to what an impartial observer would choose is something that Rawls explicitly rejects: "there is no reason why the persons in the original position

---

[38] Rawls, *A Theory of Justice*: 176.
[39] Ibid., 186.

would agree to the approvals of an impartial sympathetic spectator as the standard of justice."[40] So trustee representatives are not a satisfactory solution to identity problems in the original position.

So although the atemporal interpretation allows Rawls to avoid some of the issues raised by the PTE assumption, it is not without problems of its own—and, in particular, problems of non-identity and partiality. In this composition of the original position the parties all know themselves to be actual and not merely possible. By limiting the parties to actual people, only the interests of those who will exist are taken into account. The people who do not end up existing do not 'count'. However, the fact that those who are never born do not 'count' should be the conclusion, not built into the premises of the argument.

An Alternative Interpretation

For the sake of completeness, although Rawls does not endorse this view, I also want to consider interpretation (iii). A way of avoiding begging the question against the identities of the parties in the original position would be to stipulate that they are a sample of *possible* people from all generations. In this composition, the parties in the original position don't know whether or not they will ever actually exist, so they must reason without knowing whether they will be one of the people alive to experience the effects of the principles they choose. This interpretation eliminates what Partridge called the "unwarranted exception to the veil of ignorance"[41] and prevents possible people from being excluded.

An immediate objection to this view is similar to one of the arguments I made against trustee representatives: it would allow people who will never exist to make decisions for those who will. Since a particular person's existence is contingent on a specific combination of gametes and the number of possible combinations is so

---

[40] Ibid., 188.
[41] Partridge, "Rawls and the Duty to Posterity": 168.

vast, the number of possible people is much, much higher than the number of people who will ever actually exist. It is fair to wonder about the reasonableness of selecting principles to advance the interests of people most of whom will never actually exist. However, unlike the representatives discussed in the previous section, the possible people in the original position know there is a chance that they will come to exist and so will choose principles that *they* would be prepared to live by (or not!) once the veil is lifted. The point of the veil of ignorance is to ensure just this kind of impartiality and have people choose principles before knowing whether and/or how they will be affected by them. To extend Parfit's earlier example, it would not be a problem if, by coincidence, when the veil was lifted, all the parties ended up being men even if the principle chosen in the original position benefited women (of which there are none). Analogously, if the parties in the original position do not know if they are actual or possible people, they will choose principles impartially, and it is not a problem if those who were making the decision end up not existing.

A second objection focuses on the difficulty of conceptualising possible people in the original position. When we talk about what possible people would 'choose' or 'want', we are speaking as if they are identifiable and have interests. Yet, clearly, they are not. It stretches conceptual limitations to imagine that unborn, possible people somehow exist in some metaphysical space, waiting in the wings and hoping to be born, when in fact there *is* no 'person' to whom we can refer. The term 'possible person' refers to no one. Parfit's concern is that it would be impossible for the parties to reason without the knowledge of their own existence because "we cannot assume that in the actual history of the world, it might be true that we never exist. We therefore cannot ask what, on this assumption, it would be rational to choose."[42] Earlier I quoted Parfit's argument that it would be biased and unfair to Rawls to assume

---

[42] Parfit, *Reasons and Persons*: 392.

that the parties *do* know that they will exist. Parfit is not being inconsistent; his claim is that the original position cannot accommodate future people at all.

However, the infeasibility of conceptualising possible people is not universally shared.[43] Some people do not find it impossible to conceive of a hypothetical person and wonder what they would choose, and some philosophers write as if it is possible to think this way. Melinda Roberts, for example, asks: "Does the loss a merely possible person incurs when we leave that person out of existence altogether count against the choice that imposes that loss?"[44] Here she speaks as though the merely possible person already exists in order to incur a loss at all. I have no doubt that Roberts does not think the possible person actually exists metaphysically, just that it is possible to conceive of him or her in that way for the purposes of philosophical reasoning.

For the sake of argument, let's assume that we can imagine that the parties in the original position are merely possible and do not know if and/or when they will come to exist. What would they choose in these conditions? Tim Mulgan thinks they could go in one of two extreme directions depending on what background assumptions we make.

If we assume, realistically, that any set of future people will have some members who have lives that are not worth living because of mental or physical impairments and the like, Mulgan thinks it would be rational for the parties to choose a principle that leads to human extinction. This is because the risk-averse parties in the original position will want to minimize their chances of being born as one of these people since, *ex hypothesi*, it is bad for a person to

---

[43] Holtug, *Persons, Interests, and Justice*; N. Fotion and Jan Christian Heller (1997), *Contingent Future Persons: On the Ethics of Deciding Who Will Live, or Not, in the Future* (Kluwer Academic Publishers); Gardiner, "A Contract on Future Generations."

[44] Melinda Roberts (2010), *Abortion and the Moral Significance of Merely Possible Persons: Finding Middle Ground in Hard Cases* (Springer): 21.

come into existence with a life that is not worth living and "a rational person will prefer non-existence to a life that is not worth living."[45] If they are risk-averse, it would therefore be rational to prefer a world with *no* people to a world with many well-off people but one person with an horrendous life. But most people believe it would be somehow bad if no more humans existed—this might be because they believe it is good *for* the people who exist, because they think it is generally a good thing that people exist with good lives, or for any number of other possible reasons. Even if you are not one of those people (and I am not; more on that in Chapter 5), it is one thing for a moral theory to permit human extinction; it is quite another to say that justice requires it, as would be the case with this interpretation of the original position.

Mulgan thinks we can avoid this result only by denying that there are lives that are not worth living. Since a life worth living is something that people generally enjoy and possible people would desire, it seems reasonable to say that for the possible people in the original position existence above the threshold at which a life becomes worth living is preferable to non-existence. If a party in the original position did not know if they would exist or not, they would therefore presumably choose a principle that maximised their probability of existing as long as they were above the threshold at which a life is worth living. The best way to do so is to choose a savings principle that leads to as large a population as possible, even if this means that the average level of well-being per person decreases to just above zero—i.e., lives that are just barely worth living. In this case we end up with the repugnant conclusion: many billions of people exist with barely-worth-living lives. I suspect many people would agree with Mulgan that it is "bizarre to say that justice requires such a result!"[46]

---

[45] Tim Mulgan (2006), *Future People: A Moderate Consequentialist Account of Our Obligations to Future Generations* (Clarendon Press): 52nD.
[46] Ibid., 53nD.

While depriving the parties of the knowledge of their own existence can help us avoid non-identity and partiality problems in the original position, it has other problems of its own. For one, it would require us to suspend serious doubts about the coherence of conceiving of possible people at all and imagine that we can ask what would be in their self-interest in the original position, assuming that a possible person has a 'self' or 'interest' at all. But even if we could so conceive of possible people, what they would rationally choose does not cohere with our considered judgements about justice and population size—i.e., that justice requires neither total extinction nor the largest possible number such that everyone has a barely-worth-living life.

* * *

In my view, the foregoing discussion has shown that there's no plausible composition of the original position that avoids one or more of the following issues: introducing ad hoc elements to its structure, running afoul of the non-identity problem, or generating implausible principles of just population size. This suggests that Rawlsian contractualism is not the right kind of contractualism to derive principles of intergenerational obligations. More importantly, though, the discussion has brought to light several challenges that a contractualist approach to intergenerational justice will have to meet. First, it must avoid ad hoc motivational assumptions that explain why we choose to fulfill our obligations to the future. Second, because we will be choosing principles that will affect the identities of future people, we must determine how to contract with future people in a way that does not beg the question against their identities. Finally, and relatedly, it will have to consider the status and role of possible people—whether they are owed justification and what the implications of including or excluding them may be, especially with respect to population sizes.

Scanlon's Contractualism: What We Owe to Each Other

Those who are familiar with Scanlon's contractualism may wish to skip over this section. However, for the benefit of readers who cannot already recite passages of *What We Owe to Each Other* by heart (it's a good party trick; try it!),[47] I will outline the key elements of his theory of moral wrongness.

Like Rawls, Scanlon believes that moral principles can be produced through hypothetical agreement. Unlike Rawls, however, he does not assume mutually disinterested self-maximizers making these agreements with no knowledge of their personal circumstances. Rather, people with full knowledge of their circumstances, interests, and relationships (hypothetically) agree on a set of principles that no one could reasonably reject. But in fact, it is not quite right to say that the parties 'agree', and the name 'contractualism' is somewhat of a misnomer since actual or even hypothetical agreement does not really play a significant role. The core claim of contractualism is actually predicated not on what people would agree to, but on what people could not *reject*:

> [A]n act is wrong if its performance under the circumstances would be disallowed by any set of principles for the general regulation of behaviour that no one could reasonably reject as a basis for informed, unforced general agreement.[48]

What is key is not the descriptive question of whether people would or would not *in fact* reject certain principles, but the normative question of whether or not rejection of those principles *would be*

---

[47] Use at own risk.
[48] T. M. Scanlon (1998), *What We Owe to Each Other* (Belknap Press of Harvard University Press): 153. From this point on in the book, all references in parentheses refer to that text.

reasonable. The concept of reasonableness is doing a lot of work here. How do we know what is and is not reasonable to reject?

The Three R's: Reasons, Reasonableness, and Reasonable Rejection

Unlike the more familiar primary school three R's (reading, writing, arithmetic), contractualism's three R's actually start with 'r'—but don't get too excited; they're still slightly misnamed since there are technically four.

Reasons and Reasonableness

In everyday life, when we ask a person to 'please be reasonable!' we are asking them to take others' interests into account when forming judgements about what to do. Reasonableness can be contrasted with the concept of rationality, which Rawls describes in *A Theory of Justice* and *Political Liberalism* as acting in a way which furthers the agent's aims, preferences, or desires.[49] It is also not the same as pure altruism, in which a person primarily seeks to enhance others' abilities to pursue their own desires and preferences. Rather, it is in between these two concepts where a reasonable person pursues their aims but with a respect for the fact that he or she must take into account the interest others have in their own pursuits. Being reasonable also involves "seeing reason to exclude some considerations from the realm of relevant reasons just as it involves reasons for including others" (157). Being reasonable means not only acknowledging and caring about others' interests, but also assessing the relevance of one's own and others' reasons for acting.

---

[49] Rawls, A Theory of Justice: 143; John Rawls (2005), *Political Liberalism*, expanded ed. (Columbia University Press): 48–50.

A 'reason' is simply something that counts in favour of a particular action or belief. Scanlon argues that when we judge that a person has done something wrong, we are judging that he or she has acted on a reason that is disallowed, has given more weight to a reason than is morally permitted, or has failed to see the importance of a countervailing reason which should take precedence (201). The distinctiveness of human life is our capacity to assess reasons and justifications, so appreciating the value of others as rational beings also involves recognising their capacity to appreciate reasons.

Reasons enter the 'reasonable rejection' picture from the perspective of both the actor and the person(s) who would be affected by the action. The actor must justify their action to others (in particular those affected by a principle permitting the desired action) using acceptable reasons for why they wish to perform it. A person affected by the action in question needs to have acceptable reasons if they wish to reasonably reject a principle that permits it. Consider the example of promises. If I wish to break a promise I made to my friend to go to the cinema with her, I must be able to offer good reasons for this. Perhaps I encountered a person in need of rescue on the way, or I have caught the flu and feel too ill to go out. Likewise, I must consider what reasons she could have for rejecting a principle that allowed me to break my promise. She might, for example, have been in need of cheering up and will be very disappointed if I cancel our plans. We can act wrongly either by acting according to unacceptable reasons (reasons that are disallowed, or to which we have given too much weight), or by failing to consider the reasons that others might have to reject our action.

How do we decide which reasons can be used to reject principles and which cannot? What we can't do is appeal to a prior notion of rightness or wrongness to tell us which considerations are morally relevant and which are not. If we did so, the contractualist process would be circular since it would be the prior notion of wrongness that was doing the heavy lifting and not the notion of reasonable rejection.[50] In order to avoid this problem, there are a few specific constraints Scanlon places on what reasons are admissible. Reasons must be:

Individual
Scanlon describes as a central feature of contractualism that "the justifiability of a moral principle depends only on various individuals' reasons for objecting to that principle and alternatives to it" (229). The focus of contractualism is the standpoint of

---

[50] There are critics who make this claim. Contractualism is circular, so the objection goes, because in order to decide if a reason is admissible or not, we must already have an idea in mind of what is right or wrong. For instance, in order to hold that race (with no affirmative action objectives) is not a relevant reason to hire people, we must have already decided that hiring on the basis of race is wrong. Contractualism, on this view, presupposes some normative assumptions about what is reasonably rejectable, and thus its premises contain within them claims made in the conclusion. If we provide independent arguments for why racial discrimination is wrong, then it is those independent arguments doing the work and contractualism is redundant (also known as the 'spare-wheel objection'). See Nicholas Southwood (2010), *Contractualism and the Foundations of Morality* (Oxford University Press) and Walter Sinnott Armstrong (2006), *Moral Skepticisms* (Oxford University Press). I cannot hope to provide a full defence of contractualism against these charges here. Happily, others, including Scanlon himself, have already done so. See; Yascha Mounk (2012), "An Interview with T.M. Scanlon (Part I)," *The Utopian* (blog), https://www.the-utopian.org/T.M.-Scanlon-Interview-1 Jussi Suikkanen (2005), "Contractualist Replies to the Redundancy Objections," *Theoria* 71(1); Pamela Hieronymi (2011), "Of Metaethics and Motivation: The Appeal of Contractualism," in *Reasons and Recognition: Essays on the Philosophy of T. M. Scanlon*, ed. R. J. Wallace, Rahul Kumar, and Samuel Richard Freeman (Oxford University Press); T. M. Scanlon (2004), "Replies," in *On What We Owe to Each Other*, ed. Philip Stratton-Lake (Blackwell Press); Philip Stratton-Lake (2003), "Scanlon's Contractualism and the Redundancy Objection," *Analysis* 63(277); T. M. Scanlon (2007), "Wrongness and Reasons: A Reexamination," *Oxford Studies in Metaethics* 2: 5–20; Michael Ridge (2001), "Saving Scanlon: Contractualism and Agent-Relativity," *Journal of Political Philosophy* 9. Briefly, though, the response is that the possible reasons for rejecting principles *are* based on a prior notion, but not a notion of what is right or wrong—rather, the reason people have to want to live in a state of mutual justification. Recognising the relationship between admissible reasons and the overarching reason we have to want to justify our actions to others helps us see how contractualism avoids circularity without becoming redundant. Circularity critics argue that we must have already decided that arbitrariness was wrong in order to use it as a reason to reject a principle allowing racial hiring. Or, to avoid that, we must argue why arbitrary reasons are inadmissible, thereby making contractualism redundant. But this ignores other important questions that cannot be filled in without further explanation. What makes arbitrariness problematic? The objector cannot claim that arbitrariness itself makes principles based on it wrong without accounting for *why* this is so. Contractualism bakes the answer in by reference to its underlying justification: the reason for mutual justification and harmonious living with

individuals, not those of aggregated individuals or groups. In other words, a person must object to a principle on their own behalf, not on behalf of a group. This prevents interpersonal aggregation and ensures that a number of smaller complaints cannot outweigh a very weighty burden a single person could face. Scanlon introduces this restriction as a way of preventing some of the undesirable aspects of utilitarianism from finding their way into contractualism: "[requiring reasons to be individual] is central to the guiding idea of contractualism, and is also what enables it to provide a clear alternative to utilitarianism and other forms of consequentialism" (229). For example, a certain brand of utilitarian could argue that a healthy person ought to donate all of their organs (and by consequence their life) to save the lives of six others because the net total utility that is gained is higher than if the healthy person kept their organs and the six others died. The reason that could be offered in favour of the donation would have to be given on behalf of the six and would stem from the aggregated benefit the group would enjoy. However, contractualism would not allow the strong reason the healthy person has to want to keep their organs to be outweighed by the aggregation of each one of the six's individually smaller reasons.[51]

Personal
Personal reasons spring from things that affect persons. The most important implication of the personal reasons restriction may

---

others. Arbitrariness (and others like unfairness, discrimination, etc.) is objectionable because it's impossible to live in such a state and be governed by arbitrary principles, as these lead to people being excluded and treated without respect. The only independent assumption we need to accept is that people see reason to want to live in unity with others on reasonable terms of cooperation and mutual justification. Certain things—fairness, non-arbitrariness, non-discrimination, etc.—are necessary components of that.

[51] Some argue that this prohibition on aggregation poses problems for Scanlon, especially with regard to whether or not contractualism can justify saving the many over the few. I will discuss this debate later on in Chapter 5's discussion of optimal population size.

seem trite: impersonal reasons are not (on their own) reasons to reject a principle. The basis of contractualism is what it says on the tin: what we owe to each other—fellow persons—and not what we owe to all beings/things in the world. Impersonal reasons come from the value non-persons (e.g., objects, ideas) may have in themselves, not from their impact on persons, and so are not part of contractualism's concern and commitment to mutual respect for others. For that reason, they are not included in interpersonal justification.

This doesn't mean that impersonal reasons are completely excluded from contractualist thinking. While principles may not be rejected simply because they allow people to neglect impersonal values, genuine conflicts can arise when the principle in question *forbids* others to take particular impersonal values into account. An example Scanlon gives of such a case is a principle of fidelity to promises that would require a person to keep a promise even if it meant allowing an animal to die in pain. The animal's pain is an impersonal value,[52] but it would not be possible for a person to accept this principle and at the same time value a pain-free life for animals. Values like animal suffering are impersonal but "do bear indirectly . . . on the question of what principles we can reasonably reject, since they provide people with good reason to want to live their lives in certain ways" (222). A principle that forbade taking such values into account would prevent a person from living their life in a way that recognises certain values. He acknowledges that although the value of the animal's pain is impersonal, "there may be cases in which we have to choose between impersonal values and what we owe to each other" (223). By recognising that there can be conflicts between impersonal values and what we owe to each

---

[52] Although there is debate over the definition of 'persons' and whether animals can meet it, I shall assume, along with Scanlon, that they are not persons to whom justification is owed. This is not to say, of course, that their pain is unimportant or irrelevant; rather, it is just not part of the scope of 'what we owe to each other'.

other, Scanlon accepts that although impersonal values are not *on their own* grounds for reasonable rejection because they do not bear directly on what we owe to each other, they are still important insofar as forbidding taking them into account would prevent people from living their lives in certain important ways. Impersonal values may therefore bear indirectly on what we owe to each other, but only after being converted into personal reasons—the impact on a person's life—to reject principles (222).

Generic
Reasons must be based on commonly available information about what people have reason to want (204). When we think about whether a principle could be reasonably rejected, we must take a broader perspective than the specific individuals who will be affected by the actions licensed by the principle. Rather, we must look at the standpoint of those individuals because we cannot always know exactly which particular individuals will be affected by it and in which ways: who will benefit, be constrained, or be unaffected. The 'standpoint' is the cluster of interests, benefits, and burdens that any person who was in the position of someone affected by the principle would face. For example, if we are thinking about driving speed regulations, we must consider the standpoints of various relevant social positions like safe driver, pedestrian, and reckless driver rather than the specific individuals Jamal, Jessica, and Jared.[53]

It's important to note that generic is not the same as majority. Generic reasons need not be the reasons most people have. A small number of people could be affected by a principle that permitted agents to act in a certain way, so there could still be a generic reason to reject the principle that is based on the general characteristics of the situation if it springs from a general characteristic that

---

[53] Aaron James (2012), "Contractualism's (Not So) Slippery Slope," *Legal Theory* 18(3): 267.

these people, however few, have that is not attributed to specific individuals.

Some examples Scanlon offers of generic reasons are the strong reasons people have to want to avoid injury, rely on promises, and control what happens to their bodies (204). To this list we might add the reason to seek goods that develop personal capacities, enhance health, secure leisure time, etc. Therefore "we think it reasonable to reject principles that would leave other agents free to act against these important interests" (204).

The reason for the generic reasons restriction is that taking account of every single person's particular circumstances would be incredibly demanding and likely epistemically impossible. It would create more uncertainty and require people to gather a huge amount of information in order to know how a principle would affect every other specific individual. Furthermore, ensuring that reasons are generic makes it easier to justify reasons to others. Even if a person does not have the same reasons themselves in their personal circumstances, they can recognise that the reasons given would also be applicable to them if they were ever in the same situation.

Reasonable Rejection

To determine whether or not a principle can be reasonably rejected, we must consider the different reasons people have for rejecting the principle in question *as well as its alternatives* (213). Judgements of reasonable rejection are comparative because assessing a principle includes claiming that it is superior (or inferior) to alternative principles by showing that the objections to it are weaker (or stronger).

If we want to know if it would be wrong to perform an action A in circumstances C, we need to look at what principle P would permit such actions in these circumstances. To find out if P could be reasonably rejected, we first look at what burdens would be imposed on some people in this situation if others were permitted to do A and also what burdens would be borne by others if A were prohibited (the alternative principle) in the same circumstances. If the objections to prohibition are minor compared to the objections to permission, it is reasonable to reject P, and this means that performing A in circumstances C is wrong. Let's look at a trivial example. Some religious people might have reasons to reject a principle permitting Sunday shopping. On the other hand, secular shop owners might have a reason to reject the alternative principle (one that prohibited Sunday shopping). The job of the contractualist process is to assess the appropriateness and strength of the reasons being offered to determine whether or not the original principle could be reasonably rejected.

To reasonably reject a principle, there must be a personal, individual, and generic objection, sometimes (often?) based on the expected decrease in a person's well-being. It seems uncontroversial to accept that if complying with a moral principle would make a person's life go much worse, there are grounds for that person to object to it. However, Scanlon rejects the notion that all objections to principles must be grounded in their effect on people's wellbeing. There seem to be several reasons this is the case. First, well-being isn't easily quantitatively compared either interpersonally or intrapersonally; it is very difficult, if not impossible, to aggregate the various components of well-being and determine definitively who is better or worse off. Second, he argues that the value of things does not always derive from the fact that they make individuals better off (217–18).

It is neither necessary nor always sufficient that a principle negatively affects a person's well-being in order for it to be reasonably rejected. It is not necessary because a person could reject a principle even though it did not negatively affect his well-being. In other words, reasons other than an impact on well-being can be offered in objection to a principle. Such reasons include unfairness or arbitrariness, or other background entitlements such as rights. In James Woodward's example, a Black man is denied boarding on an airplane because of the colour of his skin. The plane ultimately crashes, killing all those on board. In this case the man's well-being was not negatively affected all things considered (in fact, he may even have been benefited), but he could still reasonably reject any principle that allowed the airline to deny him boarding on the basis of his race.[54] His objection to this principle would likely be based on the fact that it was discriminatory and arbitrary and failed to recognise him as an equal moral agent.

Furthermore, the fact that a principle would lower the well-being of a particular person is not always in itself sufficient to reasonably reject the principle if there are others who would be more seriously burdened by an alternative principle or if other people's reasons were deemed to be weightier. For example, if the enslavement of a particular race were currently permitted and a principle were considered that would prohibit it, current slave owners could not reasonably reject it simply on the basis of their reduced well-being. They would certainly be made worse off by the principle, but others (in particular, the slaves) are made much worse off by an alternative principle that permits it.

Furthermore, the way in which a burden is allocated can be grounds for reasonably rejecting the principle, even if an alternative would lead to a greater amount of burden being borne. For example, a person could reasonably reject a principle that arbitrarily (e.g., by choosing by race, gender, etc.) exempts some people from a burden borne by everyone else on the grounds that the principle treats those not exempted unfairly, even though the alternative principle would have the burden placed on everyone (211). So fewer people are burdened by the first principle, but it is rejected nonetheless since it is arbitrary and/or discriminatory. Essentially, increases or decreases in well-being can be offered as reasons in favour of or in objection to a principle, but well-being does not function as a sort of supreme value, against which all principles are evaluated. Rather, it is just one element that is drawn upon in support of or against moral principles.

---

[54] James Woodward (1986), "The Non-Identity Problem," *Ethics* 96(4): 810–11.

The Scope(s) of Contractualism

'Scope' can refer to two separate but related things:

Scope-as-sphere: what areas of morality does the theory cover?
Scope-as-agents: Who does the theory apply to?

Scope-as-sphere is about how far the sphere of morality to which we are addressing our attention extends: what questions are included? Contractualism is not an account of the whole of morality, but only the part that deals with 'what we owe to each other'. That is, how we ought to relate to others in a system of mutual recognition. This sphere includes only those components of morality that have to do with relations between persons and matters about "which we have good reason to want to be in agreement, or something close to it, with people around us" (176). The moral domain includes those questions having to do with the duties we have to other people to aid them or refrain from harming, deceiving, or coercing them, etc.

Delineating the scope of morality in this way limits what kinds of principles contractualism can yield. It means, for example, that questions regarding the obligations we have with respect to the natural environment itself (rather than the impact of the environment on people) or the treatment of non-human animals[55] cannot be answered using the contractualist framework, at least not without expanding scope-as-agents. Moreover, narrowing the moral domain to this level means that questions of personal, self-regarding morality are excluded as well. Contractualism will not have an opinion on the moral permissibility of masturbation, but it will have something to tell us about the wrongfulness of rape.

---

[55] Scanlon does suggest that a system of 'trustees' could be a way of incorporating animals into the contractualist system due to their consciousness and ability to feel pain (180–85).

This is not to say that the former question is not part of morality as it is commonly understood, but it is not the sphere of morality about which contractualism seeks to provide an explanation because it cannot be properly understood as a question of 'what we owe to each other'.

Scope-as-agents concerns to whom contractualism applies. Scanlon believes that contractualism applies to any being that can be wronged. In effect this means that contractualism applies to those to whom we can stand in the relation of mutual respect and recognition (177). More specifically, he thinks that it applies to beings who have a good, are conscious and capable of feeling pain, are capable of judging things as better or worse, and are capable of holding judgement-sensitive attitudes (179). In other words, it includes beings who are able to assess reasons and represent them in judgement and therefore those to whom we have a strong reason to want to stand in the relation of mutual respect. Scanlon acknowledges that this essentially reduces the scope of morality to adult humans with fully developed rational capacities.[56]

Next, he asks "whether morality includes within its scope all possible beings of a given kind, or only actual beings (those who do, will, or have existed), or only those beings who actually exist at the present time" (179). Briefly, because I will address this in detail in the next chapter, he believes that the idea of justifiability to all possible people seems too broad, but also that restricting morality to only presently existing people would be too narrow. His conclusion is that any actual human being (past, present, or future) provides a standpoint relative to which justifiability makes sense and therefore we have reason to value the ability to justify our actions to these

---

[56] Scanlon acknowledges the problem of children and mentally handicapped adults and addresses it with the (admittedly speciesist) comment that such people are still included within the scope of contractualism because "the mere fact a being is 'of human born' provides strong reason for according it the same status as other humans" (185).

people (186). His conclusion is that "the beings whom it is possible to wrong are all those who do, have, or will actually exist" (187).

The Appeal of Contractualism

There are a number of reasons philosophers find contractualism to be an appealing moral philosophy from a metaethical point of view: it helps us comprehend the nature of moral motivation, and it contributes to a better understanding of the nature, priority, and importance of moral reasons.[57] But I want to focus on its appealing substantive elements.

First and foremost, at its core is a fundamental respect for the value of every person. What matters to a contractualist is the effect a principle would have on each person's well-being and other aspects of a person's life. To that end, it focuses on personal and individual reasons. By limiting reasons to the individual, contractualism ensures that no person's claims are ignored, and the fundamental equality of every person is recognised. When we allow aggregation of interests, we can demand great sacrifice from one person in order to realise a greater aggregate good that nobody will actually enjoy. In contractualism people are not aggregated in order to determine the value of certain principles. Rather, each person's life and objections are taken into account.

Second, yet perhaps equally importantly, contractualism recognises the fundamental importance of the moral relationships we have to others. Scanlon takes this relationship to be central, building several aspects of the theory around the fact that we see a strong reason to want to justify our actions to others. Relationships need not involve only those with whom we have personal interactions. Rather, as moral agents, we have an intrinsic desire to justify our actions to other moral agents on the basis of their status

---

[57] Hieronymi, "Of Metaethics and Motivation."

as persons. It is an advantage of contractualism that it captures the importance of such 'otherness', rather than viewing people as extremely individualistic and self-serving.

Related to this is the fact that contractualism encourages us to step outside ourselves and consider the points of view of others in a straightforward and easy-to-understand way. Rather than focusing solely on ourselves and what is in our own interests, we balance our needs against others'. Furthermore, contractualism does this without requiring us to attempt epistemically challenging things like tallying up the total potential value or disvalue of a particular principle, or attempting to reason with no information about our personal circumstances. It does not require interpersonal deliberation or actual agreement of any kind, simply that we consider what others could reasonably reject.

Each of these virtues makes contractualism a promising theory in itself, but also one that we should consider extending to future people. Scanlon describes justifiability to others (the core of contractualism) as being basic in two ways: it "provides both the normative basis of the morality of right and wrong and the most general characterization of its content" (189). This maps clearly onto my description of the scope and content problems. If scope extends to future people (more on that later), then the justification question has been answered and we can use the contractualist method to discern the content of our obligations to them (answering the content question).

More specifically, restricting consideration to personal and individual reasons will likely stave off concerns such as the repugnant conclusion: the greater aggregate value of a larger population would not be an admissible reason since that is an impersonal value. The focus on equal moral status and respect means that it will likely not be a significant problem to explain why the theory can extend to future people since no actual interaction or reciprocity is required. Finally, since it is straightforwardly applied, it will not require us to try to guess how much value will be accumulated by various generations in different ways. It will also not require us to try to imagine what we would choose if we did not know whether and/or when we will exist, and so on, as was the case for Rawls.

Despite these promising features, there are also certain specific areas which require particular attention. First, we will need some justification for including future people in the scope of what we owe to each other. Do non-interaction, the asymmetry of power, and lack of affective ties between current and future people call into question this source of moral motivation for Scanlon? Why would people who will never meet feel any desire or reason to justify their actions to those with whom they will never interact? What about possible people? Do we need to take their interests into account and justify our actions to them in the same way we do with actual people? As we saw in the discussion of the original position, if possible people are to be excluded from the realm of what we owe to each other, this will need to be argued for and not merely assumed.

I will also need to look at what kind of reasons could be offered for or against principles that affect future people. These include the reasons future people could offer for objecting to a principle and likewise what reasons current people could use to justify their actions. The role of increased or decreased well-being as a reason for both groups is likely to be important. Furthermore, how should the reasons of future and current people be balanced when they conflict? Is there any justifiable reason to favour one group over the other or must they be treated equally? Also related to reasons, how does the personal reasons restriction influence a contractualist response to the non-identity problem since it is a particular problem for person-affecting theories?

2
Justification to Future People

I start with a possibly bold claim: when we think about what we owe to each other, we ought to include future people in 'each other'. Contractualism requires us to justify our actions to others on grounds that they could not reasonably reject. In the case of intergenerational ethics, these 'others' are the future people who would be affected by the actions we are trying to justify. Tim Mulgan argues that because contractualism is a person-affecting theory, it is prone to "all the usual difficulties facing any person-affecting theory, due to the non-identity problem and unequal circumstances."[1] I will first take up the latter part of his objection (the inequality of circumstances) and return to the non-identity problem later on. But as we have already seen, this is not the only disanalogous property that challenges the extension of ethical theories designed for contemporaries to future people. In addition to the unequal power relations to which Mulgan refers, there is also a lack of reciprocity and affective ties. It therefore seems appropriate to begin with these three properties and determine whether or not they immediately preclude the application of contractualism to the problem of intergenerational ethics. In this section I argue that they are actually quite easily accommodated.

---

[1] Tim Mulgan (2006), *Future People: A Moderate Consequentialist Account of Our Obligations to Future Generations* (Clarendon Press): 357.

Disanalogous Properties

These disanalogous properties all spring from the more fundamental problem that future people do not exist at the same time as we do. Does this rule them out as beings towards whom we owe justification? Scanlon considers in detail the creatures who might be thought to be owed justification. He divides beings into five categories, each progressively more rational:

(1) Have a good (things can go better or worse);
(2) Are conscious and capable of feeling pain;
(3) Are capable of judging things as better or worse, and more generally, capable of holding judgement-sensitive attitudes.
(4) Those who are capable of making the particular kinds of judgements involved in moral reasoning.
(5) Those beings to whom the first four criteria apply and with whom it is advantageous for us to enter into a system of mutual restraint and cooperation. (179)

He argues that justification is owed to beings in categories (3) and up but argues that in practice there is no significant difference between (3) and (4) since even group (3) does not seem to extend beyond human beings. He argues that humans' capacity for reasoning and rational self-direction calls for the kind of respect that entails treating them in ways they could not reasonably reject. We have reason to justify our actions to any human, even if they are not capable of the judgements referred to in (4).

It therefore does not seem that a lack of reciprocity or equal power relationships would preclude including future people. Depending on one's definition of reciprocity, it could mean either passive casual interaction or active cooperation for mutual advantage. I have already shown that actual interaction is not necessary under contractualism, but Scanlon also does not believe that morality needs to be mutually advantageous and explicitly excludes the features in (5) as requirements a being must have to be included in contractualist justification. For this reason, reciprocity is unnecessary and any inequality of power between parties would have no bearing on their moral obligations to each other.

To see why this is so, recall that the basis of moral motivation in contractualism is the reason we all have to justify our actions to others in a way that recognises their value as persons and to have them justify their actions to us in kind. This mutual recognition is valuable for its own sake and morality therefore extends to all those people for whom the reason to want to stand in this relation exists (178). This part of morality is not, however, intended to secure any particular benefits of cooperation. For this reason, contractualism does not require parties who are able to make and keep agreements or offer each other benefits in return for cooperation. Scanlon believes that if we insisted on limiting mutual justification to category 5, we would exclude people who cannot be restrained by moral principles and those who could not harm or benefit us and have nothing to offer by their restraint or cooperation. For example, it would exclude a homeless person with severe physical disabilities. This person has nothing of material benefit to offer me in exchange for my acting morally towards him and is incapable of harming me in any way. If morality only extended to those who can harm or benefit me by their cooperation, I would have no reason to justify my actions to this man. Yet, surely I have reason out of respect for his value as a person not to wrong him simply due to his unfortunate circumstances. In other words, because we still have reason to want our actions to be justifiable to such people, we should not require the capacities described in (5) in order for morality to apply.

What all of this means for future generations is that there is no *prima facie* reason why future people should *not* be included. The scope of justification includes all those who have or will have a good, are conscious, and are capable of feeling pain and of holding judgement-sensitive attitudes. In fact, Scanlon explicitly says so:

> [A]ny actual human being ... whether existing now or only at some point past or future time, constitutes a point of view relative to which the question of justifiability makes sense, and we have reason to value the justifiability of our actions to these people—that is to say, to those who are already dead, or are not yet born, as well as to our contemporaries. (186)

Future people are clearly among those to whom we have reason to justify our actions. It does not matter that they don't exist at the same time as we do, or interact reciprocally or on an equal footing with us. Their (future) possession of the capacities described in categories (1)–(3) gives us reason to acknowledge their value as persons and therefore to justify our actions to them. Since Scanlon explicitly denies that there needs to be reciprocal relations between parties for them to be included in the scope of what we owe to each other, the lack of such relations between generations is simply not a problem. Likewise, power relationships have no place in contractualist thought in the first place, so the asymmetrical relationship between generations in that respect is not an issue.

Consider now the final disanalogous property: the lack of affective ties. This may seem to pose more of a problem for a contractualist account of intergenerational obligations. Scanlon grounds the basis of moral motivation in the desire to live in a state of mutual recognition and justifiability. This issue is complicated by the phrasing he uses when he describes this state as 'living in harmony with others'. Why would we care about justifying our actions to people we will never meet or interact with, and how can we live in harmony with people who do not live at the same time as us?

The simple answer is that respecting the value of every person gives us reason to want to justify our actions, regardless of whether or not we will ever actually know or meet them—the very fact that they are persons of equal moral value is enough. However, this is somewhat unsatisfying on its own and requires some fleshing out. What matters in mutual recognition is that anyone at any time or place has reason to live by principles that no one could reasonably reject. There is no goal like cooperation or mutual advantage that would justify limiting the scope of those to whom justification is owed to people with whom we actually interact.[2] It is not necessary that others *know* that I am living in conformity with the requirements of principles that no one could reasonably reject because the motivation to act morally is not to make it more likely that others will relate to you in a way that respects *your* value as a person.[3] What matters is that the principles guiding your choices are justifiable to others whether or not anybody actually knows that your actions are so justifiable. There is no intended reciprocal or mutually beneficial relationship, so it is not important that we know the particular individuals to whom we are justifying our actions.

Scanlon's reference to 'living in harmony with others' is admittedly deceiving, as it does conjure up an idea of reciprocity. However, I do not believe that this was his intention given his comments earlier about not restricting the scope of justification to those who can harm or benefit us or derive some mutual advantage. Instead, I think he has in mind a mental state wherein a person feels like they have done the right thing by others in relating to them in ways that respect their moral worth. The deliberations involved in the contractualist form of moral reasoning are internal and hypothetical, not requiring any actual interaction with others to come to a conclusion about the permissibility of a particular principle. We value living in such a way that *if* we were to have a face-to-face encounter with another person, *then* we could coexist in a spirit of harmony with each other. Contractualism ensures that we do not live at loggerheads with others or in a state of conflict. Our relationship with our fellows is harmonious rather than adversarial and this applies even if we never meet, for people can live in this

---

[2] Rahul Kumar (2009), "Wronging Future People," in *Intergenerational Justice*, ed. Axel Gosseries and Lukas H. Meyer (Oxford University Press): 264.
[3] Ibid., 264.

non-adversarial way without ever meeting. This is not to say that there could not be an actual harmony as well where two people are both aware of each other's acting according to non-rejectable principles and derive positive feelings from this experience. Rather, this sort of knowledge or interaction with the people to whom you are justifying your actions is just not necessary.

How to Include Future People

So the disanalogous properties that can prevent some intragenerational theories from being straightforwardly applied to the intergenerational realm do not pose a problem for contractualism. Now that they can be put aside, let's look at the general structure of the intergenerational contractualist model.

The fact that future people do not coexist with us may not change the fact that they are owed justification, but it does raise the problem of just how we go about figuring them into our deliberations. They are not here for us to ask them what they could reasonably reject, and conditions may change dramatically over time such that it becomes difficult to predict to what a person might reasonably object one hundred years from now. One option is to adopt a trustee model whereby we take into account objections that could be raised by someone on behalf of another person. In this case, current people would act as trustees for future people's interests and raise objections on the latter's behalf. This would at least solve the problem of future people not being able to raise objections for themselves.

I am not convinced a trustee model is appropriate for two reasons. First and foremost, contractualism has never relied on an actual agreement between persons, so it is not clear why the (current) non-existence of future people would require trustees to step in to represent them. Even when we are deliberating about a principle that would affect only our contemporaries, it is not necessary that we actually *ask* a contemporary if they have any objections to it. Rather, we consider the principle from various standpoints and determine whether an individual in any of those standpoints could reasonably reject the principle under scrutiny. Obviously, it is inevitable that in the course of our lives we will meet people, discuss principles with them, and be exposed to the ideas, opinions, and objections of others. Although such actual deliberation or agreement may be fruitful, it is not a necessary component of contractualist moral reasoning. Rather, it is "hypothetical agreement which contractualism takes to be the basis of our thinking about right and wrong" (155). Since contractualism does not require actual deliberation or agreement anyway, there is nothing in its structure which precludes us from considering the standpoints of future people in exactly the same way we would with our contemporaries, without the need for a trustee model.

The second reason a trustee model is inappropriate in the case of future people is that the purpose of trusteeship, as far as Scanlon is concerned, is to represent creatures who lack the capacity to assess reasons, not people who are simply not here at the moment. Although he does not take a specific position on it, he acknowledges that a trustee model might be appropriate to represent the interests of non-human animals in order to reject principles for reasons having to do with experiential pain. However, he denies that the trustee model is needed in the case of any human beings, even those severely disabled people who are not able to develop the capacities necessary to make moral judgements. Even in such cases where they cannot understand justifications, we must still govern ourselves by principles which we believe they could not, if they did have the capacity, reasonably reject. Interestingly, he also denies that we need trustees to represent infants and children who have not yet developed the capacity for judgement-sensitive attitudes because infancy and childhood are normal stages in the progression towards becoming a being that will have the necessary capacities. As he puts it, "[T]he mere fact that a being is 'of human born' provides a strong reason for according it the same status as other humans" (185).[4] Therefore, there does not appear to be any need for contractualism to adopt a trustee model in order to accommodate future people. Rather, we can consider the interests of future people directly by considering what they could reasonably reject, not what a trustee would reject on their behalf.

Since no relevant difference between current and future people has been established, there is no basis on which to justify treating the two groups differently, or for placing a greater weight on one group's interests over another's. We must justify our actions to future people in the same way we justify our actions to our contemporaries.

To do this we must consider two points of view since the moral permissibility of an action depends not only on what others could reasonably reject but also on the reasons being used by the agent to justify the action. In the former case, a person living at T_0 needs to consider the generic reasons that may be offered against a principle by a number of other standpoints, including that of a person who will live in the future at T_1. For example, if we are considering a principle of resource depletion, we must consider the reasons future people could have to reasonably reject the principle. They might, for instance, object on the basis that it would leave them with very few resources with which to support themselves. In the latter case, the person living at T_0 must use admissible reasons to justify his actions to the people in T_1. Continuing the example of depletion, we must have good reasons to want to follow the principle. We may realize that we simply do not have enough resources to live decent lives ourselves without depleting resources. Thus, we will justify our actions to future people on the grounds that we would bear heavy burdens if we chose to conserve rather than deplete. We would then

---

[4] Scanlon acknowledges that this view is admittedly 'speciesist'. However, since the question of whether contractualism should be expanded beyond human beings is not my focus, I leave that issue to others.

have to balance the reasons against and in favour of both resource depletion and the alternative (resource conservation) to determine which principle could be reasonably rejected.

I just said we need to justify our actions with *good reasons*. What might those reasons be?

Admissible Reasons

Scanlon gives us suggestions as to what reasons might be admissible in the contractualist process of moral reasoning. I wish here to elaborate on these reasons, consider how they would work when applied to future people, and suggest some additional types of reasons that should also be allowed. As we already know, at a minimum, reasons must be personal, individual, and generic. That is, they must reflect an impact on persons, consider the interests of each individual, and apply to any person in the same standpoint—regardless of particular personal identity.

Welfare

Let's start with *welfare*. Welfare means many different things to many different people. For simplicity, I will understand it to include the degree to which a person's life has various positive material (e.g., food, shelter) and social (e.g., personal relationships, leisure time) components. Scanlon notes that the impact on welfare might well be the most likely candidate for assessing many principles, especially those of aid or rescue. The positive impact on welfare that such a principle would have for a person is an acceptable reason to use to justify the principle to others. If a person is extremely needy, in great pain, or living a barely subsistent life, it is entirely plausible to believe that their reasons for endorsing a principle of aid would be based on the positive impact it would have on their welfare.

It would also make sense to use a positive impact on welfare as a reason for justifying a less directly impactful principle like energy conservation. A current person could justify such a principle on the grounds that it improves welfare for everyone including future people since the positive health effects of burning less fossil fuel could in some cases also be felt by currently existing people.[5]

Likewise, people can use a negative impact on their welfare as a reason to reject a principle. A principle that would cause a person extreme suffering could be reasonably rejected on the grounds of the pain that person would be made to experience. In fact, welfare often has a role to play in a principle's rejectability, especially if there are alternative principles available that would not negatively impact people's welfare to the same degree. So a negative impact on welfare is an admissible reason in the contractualist formula, but as always, the impact on one person must still be balanced against the impact on others. Simply saying that a proposed principle negatively impacts your welfare does not mean that the principle can necessarily be reasonably rejected. For example, imagine principle P_1 negatively impacts Carol (a current person) in a small way. Perhaps the principle is directing her to purchase a hybrid vehicle to lower carbon emissions. The expense of purchasing the vehicle will lower her welfare slightly in that she has less money to dispose of as she pleases because the hybrid is more expensive than a conventional petrol vehicle. This is a reason she could offer in rejection of the principle. However, the only alternative principle, P_2, would leave Fred (a future person) much worse off than P_1 did Carol.[6] Perhaps this is because P_2 permits current people to drive

---

[5] For example, one study by the University of North Carolina found that curbing emissions could prevent 300,000–700,000 premature emissions-related deaths annually by the year 2030. J. Jason West et al. (2013), "Co-Benefits of Mitigating Global Greenhouse Gas Emissions for Future Air Quality and Human Health," *Nature Climate Change* 3(10).

[6] My use of proper names is simply to make the example clearer, but it is important to note that the reasons being offered must be those of a generic person in the standpoint denoted by 'Carol' or 'Fred', and not necessarily the reasons of a particular individual in a particular situation.

any vehicle they please, regardless of the emissions. This then leaves all future people, including Fred, with a highly polluted environment that negatively affects their health, income, and food security. Since contractualism calls on Carol to consider future people in her moral deliberations, she must take into account the impact that P_2 would have on Fred. Since P_2 leaves Fred much worse off than P_1 does Carol, all other things being equal, the negative impact P_1 has on her is not sufficient to reasonably reject it. Furthermore, if a proposed principle requires too great a sacrifice from one party (say, current people) relative to the benefit others would receive from the sacrifice (future people), it could also be reasonably rejected.[7] In other words, while a negative impact on welfare is an admissible reason to offer in objection to a principle, it does not necessarily make the principle automatically rejectable since the effects (having to do with welfare and otherwise) of the principle on others must also be taken into account.

Furthermore, a person could reject a principle even if it would actually *increase* his or her welfare. Put another way, a person is not *required* to accept (i.e., not reject) a principle that increases their welfare or to reject a principle that lowers their welfare. This is because non-welfare reasons may also be relevant in a particular situation. I now turn to what some of those could be.

Not-Welfare

The reasonable rejectability of a principle depends not only on the costs and burdens it imposes on persons, but also how those costs are imposed. This second set of reasons for rejection focuses on the way in which burdens are distributed. Scanlon writes that it is "sufficient ground for rejecting a principle that it singles others out,

---

[7] Leif Wenar (2003), "What We Owe to Distant Others," *Politics, Philosophy & Economics* 2(3): 287.

without justification, for a privileged moral status" (219). There are a few ways in which a principle could do this.

First, it might exempt particular people from certain moral requirements. Each of us has reason to prefer principles that favour ourselves. Oftentimes the principles that each person favours will differ or even directly clash. If a principle is made binding with no reasons other than partial reasons to support it, then one person's reason for favouring partial principles has been given precedence over another person's identical reason, without any justification (212). The person whose preferred principle is not made binding can then reasonably reject the principle that is selected on the grounds that it was arbitrary and unfair. To illustrate this point, imagine a principle governing the distribution of a generous scholarship. The scholarship can be given to either English or history students. Each type of student has a reason to want the scholarship to be given to that subject, and a reason to reject it being given to the rival subject. Assuming there are no other reasons in favour of one subject over the other, simply choosing one of the subjects over the other would be arbitrary and there would be no way to justify the principle to the students of the subject that is not selected. But there are non-arbitrary ways to choose between the subjects—we could flip a coin, for instance. Although the odds of each subject receiving the scholarship are still 50-50 either way, it would be justifiable to both sides since both could agree that the toss was done in a fair manner that was impartial to both sides.

Second, a principle could distribute benefits and burdens according to irrelevant criteria. Imagine a cooperative scheme into which everybody contributes equally with the purpose of creating benefits for all. Now imagine that we need a principle that determines how the benefits of the scheme are to be paid out. If a principle declared that the benefits ought to be distributed according to race, for instance, it could be reasonably rejected. Assuming that the purpose of the scheme is not to correct any historical or ongoing racial injustices, race is simply not a relevant criterion by which to distribute goods.

On the other hand, a principle could use acceptable reasons such as equality, need, or effort (to name just a few possibilities) to develop a fair mechanism of distribution. The difference between race and these latter types of reasons are that they are acceptable to everyone participating in the scheme as relevant to its purpose and are not merely responding to the wishes of some people (the preferred race) to benefit while neglecting the similar claims of others (the disadvantaged race). Such a principle would fail to recognise the equal moral status and rationality of all persons. So a person could reasonably reject a principle that unfairly distributed things according to irrelevant criteria even though their objection has nothing to do with the impact on welfare that the objector may experience.

A person could also reasonably reject a principle that made it impossible to recognise other important values. Scanlon's own example of this is a principle that required one to be strictly neutral with respect to friends and strangers. He thinks this would be unacceptable because it would be incompatible with the attitude and value of friendship (218–19). This is because being a friend inherently includes seeing value in the special relationship you have with your friend and reason to be partial towards them in some situations. For example, if you have only an hour of spare time on the weekend it seems reasonable for you to use that time to help your friend move house rather than helping a stranger with the same task. Strict neutrality would require something like flipping a coin to determine whom to spend your hour helping. Yet, the relationship you have with your friend gives you reason to help her rather than the stranger. A principle that is incompatible with other important values (friendship in this case) could be reasonably rejected on those grounds (220).

There are also less tangible reasons to reject a principle. Some examples that Scanlon gives are: not being able to rely on the assurances of others, having no control over what happens to one's own body, and not being able to successfully pursue important projects and relationships (204). We have good reasons to want to do all of these things, so we can make reasonable objections to principles that would inhibit them. For example, suppose a principle were proposed that sought to eliminate the human population by requiring all people to abstain from procreation (or be sterilised) but would increase each person's individual level of material welfare. Despite the increased welfare, the principle would be rejectable both on the grounds that it prevents people, both men and women, from having control over what happens to their own bodies, and because it prevents people who otherwise would have had children from pursuing this important personal project. None of these reasons are 'trumps' to other kinds of reasons—Scanlon does not believe any reasons act as trumps—but they reflect things that are important to human beings and are part of what makes life valuable to those who live it.

At this point it is worth considering whether such non-welfare-related reasons are still personal reasons and not impersonal values, which Scanlon has denied are sufficient on their own for reasonably rejecting principles. If we reject a principle because it is unfair, are we not implicitly basing this objection on the impersonal value that is 'fairness'? Likewise, in the example of a principle that makes it impossible to recognise other values such as friendship, are these reasons not based on the impersonal value of friendship, for example?

To illustrate why such reasons are still personal, consider the difference between rejecting a principle because it is unfair (allowed) and rejecting a principle simply because it would destroy an historical landmark of no importance to anyone (not allowed). In the former case, the reasons are still personal because they "have to do with the claims and status of individuals in certain positions" (219). If a person is treated unfairly, the unfairness happened *to him* as a person. *His* status as a person was questioned; *he* was treated in an arbitrary manner. On the contrary, the value of the landmark is grounded not in the claims or interests of individuals but in its alleged intrinsic impersonal value. It is therefore not included in the subject matter of *what we owe to each other*, which defines the morality important to Scanlon. By definition, impersonal reasons like the value of an inanimate object do not represent a form of concern that we owe to other individuals. Unfairness, on the other hand, does. When a person is treated unfairly, we object because we owed it to him not to treat him that way and failed. By destroying a natural landmark, we may do a wrong (in a wider sense) but we have not wronged *anyone* because the action does not have to do with our relation to other people. Other personal reasons may derive from the value that certain people find in the landmark, but it is this impact on *them* that becomes their reason for rejection, not the impersonal value of the landmark itself.

The Non-Identity Problem

Now that we have determined what kinds of reasons current and future people can use to justify or reject principles, I want to consider what is thought by some to be the most important challenge to any justification of intergenerational obligations—the non-identity problem (NIP). The NIP is a challenge to accounts of intergenerational moral obligations because it suggests that we cannot harm people in the future unless it is the case that the people who are created would have existed regardless of what actions were taken. The implicit further assumption is that if the action does not harm the person, they were not wronged. Since such surety is generally possible only in very specific circumstances, the implication is that in many cases the actions we perform cannot harm/wrong future people because they will not make them worse off, even if they have lives that are only barely worth living.

Scanlon very briefly acknowledges the NIP, saying that it is not a question of *whom* it is possible to wrong, but rather a substantive question of *when* a person has been wronged (186). While this is true, the two questions are related, and if contractualism cannot produce an example of when a future person has been wronged, it is difficult to see how future people could be considered among those whom it is possible to wrong. So the contractualist cannot ignore the NIP on the basis of this distinction alone.

In the course of examining this problem and contractualism's response to it, I will also argue that there is a specific reason that is *not* admissible in the contractualist framework: a particular person's identity or existence.

As we have seen, contractualism asks us to justify principles on grounds no one could reasonably reject. This points to two aspects of contractualism which are, essentially, two sides of the same coin. The first is to think about how a person could justify a principle to someone else—that is, what reasons can they present in favour of a particular principle and are those reasons morally allowed? "When we judge a person to have acted in a way that was morally wrong, we take her or him to have acted on a reason that is morally disallowed" (201). The second is to ask whether another person has acceptable reasons for objecting to the principle in question. The latter is what has become known as the "complaint model" of contractualism.[8] Although he has disagreed with the ways some philosophers have interpreted the complaint model, Scanlon broadly agrees that one way to think about justifiability is to look at various individuals' reasons for objecting to ('complaining about') principles and weigh them against other people's reasons (229). My suggestion is that we can use both aspects of contractualist justification (reasons presented in favour of and in objection to) to respond to the non-identity problem.

---

[8] Scanlon credits Derek Parfit with this characterisation of contractualism. T. M. Scanlon (1982), "Contractualism and Utilitarianism," in *Utilitarianism and Beyond*, ed. Amartya Sen and Bernard Williams (Cambridge University Press).

Because of its emphasis on wronging, it seems likely that any contractualist solution to the NIP will appeal to the distinction between harming and wronging. Rahul Kumar, for one, argues that within the contractualist framework of 'wronging' instead of 'harming', the non-identity problem cannot even get started. Since it is not required that an action harm a person (understood as making a person worse off) in order to be wrong, the fact that future people are not *harmed* by an action that also causes their existence does not mean that they were not *wronged* by it. This seems to be a fruitful starting point. If we agree that thinking about future people in terms of wronging instead of harming is the right way to approach the problem, we need to think about what would constitute an instance of wronging a future person. However, this is not as straightforward as it seems since some of the people to whom we are hypothetically justifying our actions will not come to exist if we perform that action.

Therefore, we have two questions to answer that broadly reflect the two aspects of contractualism that I laid out above. First, as Kumar puts it, "if the existence of the wronged is not independent of the wrongdoing, whose standing as a person was it exactly that the wrongdoer failed to appropriately take account of in her deliberations?"[9] In other words, to whom do we owe justification for moral principles, and what reasons can we offer to/for them? Second, what (if any) bearing on the reasonable rejectability of a principle does the fact that that principle caused a particular person to exist have?

Kumar's Solution

Kumar chooses to formulate his solution to the problem in the first way—by asking how current people could justify their actions to

---

[9] Kumar, "Wronging Future People," 257.

future people, despite the fact that the latter do not exist, and their identities will be dependent on the actions sanctioned by the principle in question.

Kumar believes that the best response to this problem is to appeal to 'types.' A 'type' of person is "a way of referring to a cluster of normatively significant characteristics (and relevant interests) that may aptly characterise certain actual particular individuals in actual situations."[10] When we are deciding what we owe to others, we are thinking not about particular individuals with particular personal identities, but about standpoints characterised by person types. He gives an example of the consideration an employer has to give its employees with regards to dismissal. A principle will not specify what is owed to Sarah, a particular employee with a token identity; rather, it specifies what is owed to a particular type description—being an employee at risk of termination. Every individual will simultaneously be a part of many different type descriptions—student, employee, mother, daughter, and so on. The identity of a person is irrelevant when determining what is owed in a particular situation—any individual fitting the relevant type description in that situation will be owed the same.

For this reason, Kumar thinks contractualism is immune to the non-identity problem. This is because in the same way that an employer developing office policies does not give consideration to particular employees with particular identities, current people do not give consideration to particular future people. Kumar's argument is that if an individual comes into existence with a cluster of interests constitutive of a type, and we take that standpoint into consideration in our deliberations about a principle, then we have fulfilled the requirements of contractualist justification, regardless of whether it was also that principle that caused the person to exist. If we do not, we have wronged them.

---

[10] Ibid., 261.

There is a lot to like in Kumar's view, and while I agree with his strategy and conclusion, I think there is a potential objection that he has overlooked along the way. This doesn't mean his strategy fails, because I think that by identifying and responding to this objection, we can ultimately strengthen Kumar's argument. Along the way we will also find that personal existence is not an admissible reason within the contractualist framework, and that possible people are not owed justification. This conclusion will have several important implications relevant to the non-identity problem, but also to multiple other issues to come in later chapters.

The objection I have in mind is the following: shouldn't personal existence be considered one of the interests in the cluster of interests that is represented by a particular standpoint or type? The claim would be that people have an interest in existing and this interest should be part of any future person's standpoint. The consequence is that when we consider how a principle would affect a particular type or standpoint we must include the interest in existing as part of that standpoint and consider that any person represented by the standpoint might reasonably reject a principle that prevents their own existence. This would work in the same way as any other interest that may be part of the standpoint. For example, if a principle would cause a person bodily harm, and they have an interest in avoiding such harm, the fact that this interest is part of the cluster in the standpoint gives them reason to reject the principle.

To see how this works, imagine Hilary is considering whether or not she should conceive a child in the summer despite knowing that any child she conceived at that time would be born blind. Contractualism requires her to consider whether the resulting child could reasonably reject a principle that permitted her to conceive in the summer, despite knowing they would be born blind. The child in question, Ian, could potentially reasonably reject the principle on the grounds that he will be burdened with blindness; but if Ian does reject it, *he* will never exist. So, upon reflection, Hilary decides that Ian could not reasonably reject a principle allowing her to conceive him knowing he will be blind, because if he did, he would never exist. He is therefore not wronged by her choice to conceive him despite the fact that he is born blind. This is the same conclusion as the non-identity problem.

However, I argue that this is not the case and that the interest in existing is not properly included as part of such a standpoint. Rather, it is a basic requirement for being in a position to occupy a standpoint at all. Allowing (non-)existence to be the basis for rejecting a principle is tantamount to including possible people in the scope of those to whom we owe justification because the only people who could reject a principle on the grounds that it prevented them in particular from existing are those who could have but do not exist (i.e., possible people). However, to avoid one of the same criticisms I levelled at Rawls, excluding existence as a component of a standpoint, and therefore also excluding possible people, cannot just be baked in, but needs defence.

The first argument against the inclusion of existence in a standpoint is that it is incoherent since it would require people to justify their actions to unreal standpoints. Non-existence is not a standpoint; by definition no one can occupy it. If it were a standpoint, we would have to think of a world full of possible people waiting in the wings whose existence would have been fixed were it not for our performing a certain action which prevented their existence. This seems implausible to me. Scanlon himself admits that conceiving of justification to all possible people is barely coherent at best (186). He says that we can only wrong a person who has, does, or will exist because wronging involves failing to take another person's interests into account. Even if there is an interest in existence (which I deny), we cannot take a possible person's interest in existing into account because 'they' do not exist if we follow whatever principle we are proposing. By considering the standpoint of a person in our deliberations, we consider the burdens they will have to bear as a result of the principle. However, only people who exist can bear the brunt of a principle and therefore occupy a standpoint.

Second, but related, is that existence is not an interest at all, and a possible person is not disadvantaged by never existing. Rather than being an interest itself, existence is a necessary requirement in order to have interests in the first place. Rivka Weinberg describes it as 'neutral' because causing a person to exist is to create a subject who can have interests and not an interest itself. In order to be disadvantaged, there must be some detrimental effect on your interests. However, without existence, a person does not have any interests, so they cannot be disadvantaged by being kept out of existence. But as Weinberg points out, "never having interests itself could not be contrary to people's interests since without interest bearers, there can be no 'they' for it to be bad for."[11] So a principle that results in some possible people never becoming actual does not impose any costs on those 'people' because nobody is disadvantaged by not coming into existence. Since existence is not an interest, it cannot be one of the cluster of interests that constitutes a standpoint.

Finally, and more practically, that a principle bears on whether a particular person exists or not cannot be part of a standpoint and therefore admissible grounds for rejecting or justifying a principle since any principle will cause a set of people to exist and another set not to exist. Allowing (non-)existence into the framework would mean that any conceivable principle could theoretically be reasonably rejected by someone. Since different actions will lead to different sets of individuals existing, a principle that permitted a certain (otherwise innocuous) action could be reasonably rejected by the people whom it prevented from existing. Likewise, its alternative, a principle that prohibited the same action, could be reasonably rejected by the people who would have been born if the action had been permitted. Imagine S_A is the set of people who will be created by principle A (P_A) and S_B is the set of people created by the alternative, principle B (P_B). S_B could reasonably reject P_A since it

---

[11] Rivka M. Weinberg (2008), "Identifying and Dissolving the Non-Identity Problem," *Philosophical Studies* 137: 13.

would cause them never to exist. Likewise, S_A could reasonably reject P_B since it would cause *them* never to exist. So a situation arises where both principles could be reasonably rejected and we are not permitted to follow either principle. Principles allowing us to carry out everyday activities like travelling, joining clubs, or taking walks could be rejected if they would lead to a course of events that prevented a particular future person from being conceived. Since virtually every action and decision we make influences who in particular will be born, we would essentially be morally paralyzed and even basic, everyday activities would be morally wrong since they prevented certain people from coming to exist.

Of course, this point on its own is not enough to show that personal existence should not be included in standpoints. An objector could claim that the fact that contractualism cannot elicit any non-rejectable principles (assuming the fact that a principle would result/not result in a person's existence were allowed as the basis for reasonably rejecting a principle) shows that contractualism cannot cope with intergenerational problems at all. However, given that there are at least two other reasons for excluding personal existence from standpoints, it is plausible to see this implication as an argument against allowing someone to reject a principle on the grounds that realizing it would result in their non-existence, rather than as an argument against contractualism itself.

Arguing that the fact that following a given principle affects whether a person is born or not is not an admissible reason for that person is not to discount it as a reason at all, or to claim that it is not something that people find important to them. It is just not an allowable *moral* reason. By 'moral reason' I mean a reason that is deemed to be relevant in the course of deliberations about what we owe to each other. There are plenty of other reasons that are not moral in this sense. Impersonal reasons may fall into this category, as might reasons like selfishness. We have reason to act selfishly in the sense that it might further our self-interest in some way to do so. But non-moral reasons such as these are considerations which provide "no justification for action in some situations even though they involve elements which, in other contexts, would be relevant" (156). It is entirely possible that existence could be relevant in many different contexts, even if not with respect to what we owe to future people.

Justification to Future People

We have now seen that a particular person's existence is not properly included in a type or standpoint and that we do not owe justification to merely possible people. What implications does that have for the non-identity problem?

Most attempts to solve the non-identity problem focus on what people in the future (once they exist) would say about what their ancestors chose to do. Would they regret their ancestors' actions even though it was those very actions that caused them to exist? There are good reasons for the dominance of this *ex post* perspective. Future people are the ones affected by our actions and bear the burdens of our choices, so it makes sense to think about how they are affected by them. However, rather than only thinking about the problem from the perspective of a person looking backwards reflecting on their actual circumstances, we should also look at it from our perspective looking forwards when deciding what we should do.

Contractualism is comparative, meaning that we have to look not only at what reasons others (for our purposes, in the future) might have to object to principles, but also at the reasons we can offer in favour of the principles we wish to follow. We must ask ourselves whether or not the reasons we offer in support of our favoured principles enable us to relate to future people in a way that respects their value as persons.

Can the fact that a principle caused a person to exist be a reason used to justify a principle to a future person's standpoint? Some might argue that we could justify the principle to that standpoint by saying something along the following lines: 'Look, if I don't do A, you'll never exist. Since you have an interest in existing, I can justify a principle that permits me to A on the grounds that it will cause you to exist. I have therefore taken your interest into account in my deliberations about the principle, and even though my doing A causes you to have a barely-worth-living life, I have not wronged you.' I argue that this view is mistaken because claiming that a principle will cause a particular person's existence is not sufficient to justify the principle to that person.

As we know, being moral involves seeing certain reasons as excluded from the realm of moral decision-making and others as included. This means that certain reasons do not qualify as reasons that can be used to justify principles to others. But how do we know when a reason is disallowed or given more weight than is permissible? There are no hard-and-fast rules and we must make our own judgements, but an initial answer to this question must call upon the source of moral motivation in contractualism: a reason is inadmissible if it does not accord with these aim of living in unity with others and respecting their values as persons. Imagine I walk past a stranger lying seriously injured on the street because I am simply too lazy to stop and help him. I have acted wrongly not only because he could reasonably reject a principle that allowed me to ignore him, but *also* because I cannot justify my actions (or, more precisely, a principle that permits my actions) with good reasons. I have no acceptable reason for walking past. I am not on my way to help someone else, I am not injured myself, and it would take very little of my own time and effort to at least call an ambulance for him. I have failed to recognize that his strong interest in being assisted countervails my interest in being lazy. Consequently, I have not related to him in a way that respects his value as a person and I have wronged him. This failing makes it impossible for him to feel unity with me, which is why my reasons in this situation are disallowed.

The same framework can be applied to decisions current people make that will affect future people, such as Parfit's *Depletion/Conservation* example.[12] We must ask whether the reasons current people have for choosing either the *Depletion* or *Conservation* policy are justifiable. The difference between this kind of decision and helping the stranger lying in the street is that *Depletion* will cause certain people to exist, and some might think that current people could justify choosing *Depletion* on the grounds that it will cause those people in particular to exist.

As I argued earlier, personal existence is not a relevant reason in the contractualist framework. Therefore, just as it (or rather, a lack of it) cannot be used as a reason to reject a principle, it also cannot be used to justify one's actions to another person. However, even if it could, unless creating that particular person is the reason for action, the action could still not be justified on the basis of creating a particular person. Although we may create *somebody*, we have no control over the particular people who are created, and the reasons used to justify the principle cannot be the creation of a particular person or set of persons.

Jeff McMahan agrees, saying that if one chooses to cause an individual to exist, that may be good for the individual who comes to exist, but it cannot be one's reason for acting, to bestow that good on that individual.[13] Since we cannot know when we are deciding on a principle now which particular future people will be created and with what identities, the assessment of our reasons for action cannot be based on these particular individuals and the fact that they either will or will not be created. So creating particular people cannot be a reason in favour of the principle and the principle needs to be justified on the basis of another reason.

---

[12] Derek Parfit (1984), *Reasons and Persons* (Oxford University Press): sec. 4.
[13] Jeff McMahan (1981), "Asymmetries in the Morality of Causing People to Exist," in *Harming Future Persons: Ethics, Genetics and the Non-Identity Problem*, ed. Melinda A. Roberts and David Wasserman (Springer): 52.

In a case like *Depletion*, the reason for our action is self-interest, which is unlikely to outweigh the burdens that would be characteristic of the standpoint of future people living in a resource-depleted world, whoever in particular they may be. Our own gain at the expense of others is not an acceptable reason under contractualism, as it would be arbitrary. Instead, we must "rely on commonly available information about what people have reason to want" (204). In this example, we can be reasonably certain that people in the future will have reason to want, at the very least, a decent quantity of resources (for example) in order to work, be productive, and live worthwhile lives. Knowingly depleting resources and creating people who will have barely-worth-living lives shows a fundamental disregard for the value of those people, even if the depletion was necessary for their existence.

The Complaint Model—What Can Future People Reasonably Reject?

So far I have shown that the fact that a principle would create a particular person or set of persons cannot be a reason in *favour* of that principle. Now I will consider the other side of the justificatory coin and look at whether existence factors into reasons to *object* to principles. I will argue that the fact that a principle leads to a particular person's existence does not mean that that person has no reason to reject it. In other words, I will defend the claim that a person can reasonably reject a principle even though it caused them to exist.

In his discussion of contractualism and the non-identity problem in *On What Matters*, Parfit argues that when we can avoid creating people with bad lives at little cost to ourselves, it would be wrong not to. However, if we act in these ways, certain future people will never exist. He believes that when we apply Scanlon's contractualism in a way that appeals only to personal reasons, we are forced to ignore the fact that if we had acted differently, a different set of people would have existed and been much better off.[14] He thinks that in order to appeal to these facts, Scanlon must revise his claims about impersonal reasons as admissible grounds for rejecting principles. Parfit argues that in order "to explain why certain acts or policies would be wrong, we must appeal to the better lives that would have been lived by the people who, if we had acted differently, would have later existed."[15] He agrees that being caused not to exist cannot be a reason to reject a principle, but concludes from this fact that we need to appeal to the impersonal reasons that are held by the people who do end up existing. The thought seems to be that if you are caused to exist, you do not have a personal reason to reject the principle that led to your existence but there is still an impersonal reason to create a better life instead. Because of this, Parfit argues, we need to admit impersonal reasons in order to explain why such principles could be reasonably rejected.[16]

In making the argument that a principle causing a person to exist necessarily precludes the person from rejecting it, Parfit seems to be assuming that existence is the only morally relevant factor (or at least the most important factor) in evaluating principles and negates any other facts about a situation or standpoint. In examining a case in which a particular person (Charles) would not exist if a principle were followed, Parfit says that if we had chosen that principle, Charles would have no reason to reject it, even though the principle left him with a low quality of life.[17] In Parfit's view, if a person is caused to exist with a life worth living because of a principle, they can never have a personal reason to reject that principle since existence automatically outweighs any other burdens the person may bear as a result of the principle. He believes that in order to avoid the non-identity problem, contractualist objections to a principle

---

[14] Derek Parfit (2011), *On What Matters*, vol. 2 (Oxford University Press): 235.
[15] Ibid., 239.
[16] Ibid., 239–40.
[17] Ibid., 236.

must be made on the basis that a different principle would have led to better lives being lived by other people (an impersonal reason).

I do not agree that contractualism has this implication. Rather, the objections to the principle could be based on any number of other factors relevant to the standpoint of the actual people who exist as a result of it, not on the basis of the impersonal value of other, better lives that could have been lived as a result of an alternative principle. In fact, I will argue that a future person could have personal reasons to reject a principle that caused them to exist with a life worth living if the principle imposed other costs on them.

Assuming that a person could not reasonably reject a principle that caused them to exist is to prioritize existence over all other things. Imagine a principle that caused a child to exist with a severe disability and a life barely worth living. Assuming that existence outweighs all other considerations is also to argue that it is in the interest of the future person to have a disability if the only way they could have existed is to have that disability. And further, it is also to argue that it is in a possible person's interest to have a disability in order to "secure the good of existence" since the person could not exist without the disability. However, it cannot be in a possible person's interest to either exist or to have a disability since they do not have interests. Weinberg argues, I think correctly, that we should not ask how future people can rationally object to principles that caused them to exist; rather, we ought to take existence as a given and ask whether they could reasonably reject the circumstances in which they do exist.[18]

If we take it as a given that a person exists, there are many things that affect their quality of life, including their health, physical environment, and so on. Everyone, regardless of their particular identity, has reason to want to have at least adequate resources to support themselves. If *Depletion* is chosen, people A will be created who live low qualities of life due to the lack of resources. The principle could

[18] Weinberg, "Identifying and Dissolving the Non-Identity Problem": 15.

be reasonably rejected by people A on the grounds that it left them without sufficient resources to ensure a decent quality of life. Since anyone in people A's standpoint would have a generic reason to want to have a good enough quality of life, they could reasonably reject a principle that allows *Depletion*.

I have argued that existence is not an interest a person has and is therefore not part of the standpoint to which we owe justification. However, one might disagree and say that a life (even barely) worth living by definition counts as good for the person living it. The critic might wonder how a barely-worth-living life could itself count as an objection. So for now, let's allow that existence *does* improve a person's well-being and is good for that person. I think that even in that case, a person could still reasonably reject a principle that caused them to exist with various elements that constitute a very low quality of life.

In this scenario, because existence is assumed to improve well-being, it could be argued that people A would have a reason to accept the principle that allows *Depletion* because without it, they would never have existed. The reasons of existence and the desire to have ample resources conflict. People A therefore have both a reason to reject the principle and a reason to accept it, and these reasons need to be balanced against each other. But remember that the key point in contractualism is what people *could* reasonably reject, not whether or not they actually *would*. A person can reject a principle even if it increases her well-being or not reject one that decreases her well-being (213–16). In other words, we aren't required to accept (i.e., not reject) principles just because they increase our well-being or to reject ones because they decrease our well-being. A significant decrease in well-being *can* be a relevant reason for rejection, but it is not necessary. A principle that increases a person's well-being could also be rejected on other grounds. For example, a principle allowing the enslavement of a particular race would certainly increase the well-being of a person who would benefit from slave labour. However, that same person could still reasonably reject the principle on the grounds that it was unfair and/or discriminatory. Recall Woodward's example of Jones, a Black man who is denied boarding on an airplane by a racist cabin crew.[19] The plane ultimately crashes, killing everyone on board. Jones is counterfactually made better off by the crew—if he had been allowed on board, he'd have died. But he still has reason to complain about the racist discrimination he encountered. Jones can reasonably reject a principle allowing Black people to be denied boarding from airplanes, even though the principle would ultimately make him better off, because the principle is unfair.

Reasons and judgements about reasons can and do conflict, and there is no reason to lament this (28). It is not for us to speculate about how people A would balance their well-being gained from existence against their reason to want a good environment in which to live. What is important is that the reason for wanting sufficient environmental resources is enough to say that people A *could* reasonably reject the principle allowing *Depletion* on that grounds.

But it might also be objected that simply having a low quality of life does not give you a claim against the person who created you. It is true that, as David Benatar has famously argued, every life will inevitably include some negative elements and harms. Furthermore, it would seem that if we did agree that any kind of low quality of life gave a person reason to reject their creation, most people who have ever lived will have been wronged. Living standards in the past were much lower than they are today, and it stands to reason that the low qualities of life lived by people in the past would have given them reason to reject principles leading to their creation. However, it does not seem plausible (*contra* Benatar) to say that every person past or present could object to a principle permitting their creation on the grounds that they have some negative element in their life. The question is, then, how bad must a life be in order for the

---

[19] James Woodward (1986), "The Non-Identity Problem," *Ethics* 96(4).

principle permitting its creation to be non-rejectable? This is a question that I will take up in detail in the next chapter. For now, however, my aim has simply been to show that it is possible that a person could reasonably reject a principle even if that same principle resulted in their own existence.

Putting It All Together

Putting the arguments together, it is clearer how contractualism copes with the non-identity problem. If a principle permits the creation of a person with a barely-worth-living life, the person who is created has grounds for rejecting that principle. On the flip side, no one has a reason to reject a principle that would prohibit the creation of a person with a barely-worth-living life because the only 'burden' of prohibition would be 'felt' by those who never exist—i.e., the 'people' with barely-worth-living lives who would have been created if it were not morally impermissible. Because possible people are not owed justification, this cannot be a reason to reject a principle. Furthermore, there are no countervailing reasons in favour of permission that would overcome the burdens suffered by people who do come to exist with barely-worth-living lives, since it was shown that the reason in favour of such a principle (that it creates particular people) is not an allowed reason.

Ultimately, the contractualist response to the non-identity problem rests on two primary claims that I have defended. First, current people cannot justify principles to future people simply by appealing to the fact that that principle also caused those future people to exist. Second, a person can reasonably reject a principle even though it caused them to exist if there are other grounds for objection—i.e., the fact that a principle caused them to exist does not mean that they must accept it, or, more precisely, that they have no reason to reject it.

An important implication of the previous discussion will form the basis of several arguments I make in the coming chapters. Since we have established that a particular person's existence is not properly included in the standpoint to which we are justifying our actions, a future 'person' could not reject a principle on the grounds that it prevented his or her existence. This means that when we are considering who could reasonably reject a principle, we need not consider the interests of merely possible people. For example, imagine we are considering a principle of *Conservation* whereby current people conserve resources in order to pass on to the future as much or more than they received from their predecessors. We must ask what reasons current and future people could have to reasonably reject the principle. The future people who will exist under *Conservation* would likely have no reason to reject the principle since they will be left with ample resources with which to maximise their quality of life. The possible people who will be caused not to exist under *Conservation* would presumably want to reject the principle since it leads to their non-existence. However, the fact that a principle causes them to exist or causes them not to exist is not a grounds for reasonably rejecting a principle and so their claims should not be included. This amounts to not considering possible people at all. The effects a policy would have on possible people cannot present an objection to anything since by definition there are no such people and no such effects. *Conservation* could therefore not be reasonably rejected by future people[20] and, barring any reasons current people might have to reasonably reject it, it would not be wrong to conserve resources: "we cannot defensibly claim that some act is wrong because any principle that permits such acts could be reasonably rejected by people who never exist."[21]

---

[20] I assume that the future people who do exist will not have to bear any burdens because of *Conservation*.

[21] Parfit, *On What Matters*: 234.

This chapter has focused on the scope problem. That is, I aimed to justify the existence of intergenerational obligations generally, and the inclusion of future people in the realm of what we owe to each other in particular. From this point on, I will be taking up the book's title question and trying to answer the content problem: *what do we owe future people?*

3

Intergenerational Resource Distribution

This chapter answers one component of the content question: how much must we conserve for future generations? Whilst the substantive focus of this chapter is on resources, the concept of 'reason-balanced sufficientarianism' that I will develop here will also play a significant role in the next two chapters on procreation and optimal population size.

What Are We Distributing and Why?

Before we can even start to wonder *how much* we owe future generations, we need to know what we are talking about and why. There are a variety of opinions about what people are entitled to—certain levels of welfare, resources, opportunities, etc. For my purposes, I will understand the purpose of intergenerational distribution as being to secure for future people a particular quality of life; what that level should be is the focus of this chapter. Quality of life is determined by the quality of the social and material conditions someone enjoys, including nutrition, protection against illness, personal security, autonomy, negative freedoms, and opportunities for education and leisure time. More precisely, the purpose of intergenerational distribution is to provide future people with the *opportunity* for a particular quality of life. This is because future people will exist in the future and we will have no way of providing extra resources if they are not able to enjoy the quality of life justice demands, either because they chose to squander resources or because they suffer an unfortunate natural disaster that we could not possibly have foreseen and can, at this point, do nothing to prevent or alleviate. I believe that conceiving of our duties in terms of *opportunity* for quality of life best accommodates the temporal gap between current and future people.

The most straightforward way the current generation can provide opportunities for quality of life to future people is by leaving resources for them to use. I have in mind several different types of 'resource'. First, renewable or non-renewable natural resources like crude oil, minerals, and arable land are things that people use to develop and run technology, produce food, and create shelter (among other things). There are also many non-natural, tangible resources such as technology and infrastructure like schools, hospitals, etc. Intangible resources include cultural traditions, knowledge, language, and institutions such as the judicial system or United Nations. In addition, there are things that are resources in the sense that they provide the conditions that facilitate the use of other resources; examples include clean air and water, and a healthy environment generally. The quantity and quality of each type of resource available impact a generation's opportunity to enjoy a high quality of life.

Some brief points before moving on. First, when we talk about what the current generation owes to future generations, we refer to 'us' and 'them' as if they were individual actors, when of course they are actually collectives of very many actors including states, nations, and individuals. For the purposes of this chapter, though, I will ignore this complication and treat generations as individual, homogenous entities. I will also ignore the fact that within any given generation there will be members with much higher qualities of life than others.[1]

---

[1] I discuss this problem in Elizabeth Finneron-Burns (2023), "Global Justice, Sovereign Wealth Funds, and Saving for the Future," *Critical Review of International Social and Political Philosophy*. Online First.

How Should We Distribute Intergenerationally?

There are a variety of different possible accounts of how much we ought to save for the future. Some might believe that we ought to ensure that future people are at least as well off as we are, while others argue that our obligation is to leave future generations with a sufficiently good life (however that is defined). I will consider both of these positions, arguing that neither fully captures what we owe to future people. I then develop what I believe to be a more plausible set of principles of resource conservation that contractualism would endorse, what I call 'reason-balanced sufficientarianism'.

Intergenerational Egalitarianism

One view could be that we are required to leave future generations with the opportunity to have a quality of life equal to that of the current generation. There are non-intrinsic and intrinsic reasons to value equality.[2] The question is whether contractualism would endorse either type in the intergenerational context.

Scanlon's Non-Intrinsic Egalitarianism

What sorts of reasons might a person have to object to inequality? Unlike some of the topics to come, Scanlon does directly address this question in his book *Why Does Inequality Matter?* He gives us six reasons to care about material inequality:

(1) *Status.* Inequality creates humiliating differences in status.
(2) *Control.* Inequality gives the rich unacceptable forms of power over those who have less.

---

[2] See Martin O'Neill (2008), "What Should Egalitarians Believe?," *Philosophy & Public Affairs* 36(2) for a nice mapping of the terrain and clear distinctions between telic, deontic, and non-intrinsic forms of egalitarianism.

(3) *Opportunity*. Economic inequality undermines equality of opportunity.
(4) *Political Fairness*. Inequality undermines the fairness of political institutions.
(5) *Equal Benefits*. Inequality results from violation of a requirement of equal concern for the interests of those to whom the government is obligated to provide some benefit.
(6) *Unfair Economic Institutions*. Inequality of income and wealth arise from economic institutions that are unfair.[3]

Scanlon recognises that these objections to inequality "presuppose some form of relationship or interaction between the unequal parties . . . [such] objections thus do not apply to people who have no interaction with one another."[4] Do non-overlapping generations interact or have a relationship with each other in the relevant way that generates these objections to inequality?

What Scanlon means by *Status* is that under economic inequality, the poor have "to live and to present oneself in a way that is so far below the standard generally accepted in the society that it marks one as inferior."[5] This means that inequalities so great that they cause unworkably poor relationships between citizens, such that there is no basis for mutual respect between the parties, are morally objectionable. Among contemporaries, this would surely be a concern. However, it is difficult to see how humiliating differences of status would occur intergenerationally when the non-overlapping generations do not interact. Being humiliated by differences in material well-being requires more than just knowing that someone is better off than you are. Rather, it requires some sort of negative social environment that is produced by the unequal circumstances and unequal interactions between the better-off person and the

---

[3] T. M. Scanlon (2018), *Why Does Inequality Matter?* (Oxford University Press): 8–9.
[4] Scanlon *Why Does Inequality Matter?*: 9.
[5] Ibid., 5.

worse-off person in order to make the worse-off person feel inferior. This is not possible with non-overlapping generations, so this particular reason for equality is not applicable.

The objections to *Control* are predicated on the reasons people have to want to avoid being controlled by others. Economic inequality means that some people in society hold most of the wealth, giving them control over others—where and how they work and earn money, what they can buy, and generally how their lives go.[6] When people have fewer resources, they also have fewer life opportunities and options and are often forced to accept unfair terms of cooperation such as working for extremely low wages if no other jobs are available. The better-off are therefore able to take advantage of the worse-off and treat them unfairly. The direction of travel is important here. Scanlon's claim is that inequality leads to control/power over others. In the intergenerational context, earlier generations control later ones, but it is not because of unequal distributions between them, but because of 'time's arrow'. Earlier generations will always exercise a significant amount of power and control over future generations, and this isn't exacerbated by earlier generations having more material wealth. For the same reason, later generations being significantly better off than their predecessors in no way gives them any power to control those who have come before them. There's no objection to intergenerational inequality on the basis of *Control*.

A potential objection to my argument that the reasons of *Status* and *Control* do not apply intergenerationally could be that I have focused exclusively on non-overlapping generations and ignored the fact that generations do not exist in isolated cohorts, but rather overlap with each other. If Generations A and B overlap, and Generations B and C overlap, then there is a case for equality between A/B and between B/C on the grounds of *Status* and *Control* and therefore also for equality between A/C, and so on down the

[6] Ibid., 6.

line. However, even looking at it this way would allow significant inequalities between distant generations. The arguments from *Status* and *Control* do not require absolute equality between parties; they require only that inequalities between them not be so vast as to create situations in which the worse-off feel humiliated, or are dominated by the better-off. This means that Generation B could be somewhat better off than Generation A, and Generation C could be somewhat better off than Generation B. This would be unobjectionable because these small inequalities would not be enough to generate *Status* or *Control* problems between the overlapping generations. However, these small differences accumulate over time to create great differences between Generation A and Generation H who will never overlap or interact. In the unlikely case that Generations A and B were wildly unequal, *Status* or *Control* could be reasons to reject that inequality, but in the far more likely scenario where the inequalities between overlapping generations are relatively small, contractualism would still nonetheless not require intergenerational inequality, and either way there would be no objection to inequality between non-overlapping generations.

The third and fourth reasons for favouring equality, *Opportunity* and *Political Fairness*, are based, respectively, on the reasons people have to want to be able to compete on fair terms for economic advantage or to play a role in the process through which their society is governed. Everyone has an interest in their political institutions being fair so that their relationship with fellow citizens is of a desirable character. Furthermore, people have an interest in ensuring that whatever they gain from political institutions will be fairly gained and therefore legitimate. If economic inequality gives extra opportunities to some, and/or renders political institutions unfair, then this influence is illegitimate. This is a deontic reason to care about equality and requires more than just basic social interaction. It requires an institutional setting that can both be fair and enforce fairness. It is therefore an even less likely candidate to justify intergenerational equality because there are no institutions that govern intergenerational relations and procedures.

Scanlon gives some concrete examples of how inequality might affect procedural fairness. First, inequality in family income might affect a person's prospects of success in the market (*Opportunity*). Among contemporaries, it might be economic inequality itself that is causing some people not to benefit, but between generations it is unclear how unequal circumstances could impact a person's prospects of success. Second, inequality allows the wealthy to be able to gain political office and influence in a way the worse-off cannot (*Political Fairness*). This problem is inapplicable intergenerationally in the same way *Control* was. Economic inequality itself does not give one generation the ability to affect institutions in a way that would produce procedural unfairness.

Scanlon's fifth reason, *Equal Concern*, is based on the assumption that if each member of a cooperative group has a claim to equal benefits, then absent any special justifications, they ought to be provided with that benefit equally by the institution responsible for distributing the benefit in question. For example, if the government is required to provide health care to all citizens, it would be unfair if some geographical areas received better care than others. Every citizen, qua citizen, has an equal claim to health care services, so inequality based on location (like the 'post code lottery' in the United Kingdom[7]) is unacceptable. However, as Martin O'Neill notes, this reason for equality "gets its purchase in contexts where there is some distributive agency that falls under an independent obligation to provide some good among the members of

---

[7] The UK's 'post code lottery' refers to variations in availability and quality of health care between different geographical areas in the UK that are arbitrary and unrelated to need. Differences in outcomes for cardiac arrest and cancer, access to surgery, and presence of preventive health measures have all been found to differ by location, even once controlling for other factors. Clare Graley, Katherine May, and David McCoy (2011), "Postcode Lotteries in Public Health—The NHS Health Checks Programme in North West London," *BMC Public Health* 11.

a particular population."[8] When these conditions obtain and the agency in question fails to provide equal benefits, this constitutes an objectionable inequality. However, there is no intergenerational distributive authority, even among members of the same political community. Among contemporaries, the state is the primary distributive agent. Its responsibilities include health care but also extend to other services such as roads and education. The state is not, however, responsible for distributing these goods directly to future generations since future people do not exist in a reciprocal relationship with current people. The state may choose to earmark goods for future generations or have an effect on the ability of future states to distribute such goods, but the state's role is not to directly distribute them to future people. Therefore, future people cannot be said to have an equal claim to benefits from the current state, and this reason for equality does not apply intergenerationally.

Scanlon's final reason is *Unfair Economic Institutions*. Inequality is objectionable when it arises from institutions that are unfair insofar as "unequal rewards are assigned to certain economic roles or positions."[9] By definition, this reason relies on shared economic institutions. It is doubtful that non-overlapping generations share an economic system since an economy requires two or more agents producing, consuming, and exchanging goods/services to operate. In other words, the agents must interact. Furthermore, even if it could be argued that non-overlapping generations shared economic institutions, in order for any inequality between generations to be unjust, it must be the case that higher rewards were being assigned to the roles performed by one generation over another. This seems unlikely. Finally, this reason to care about inequality, even among contemporaries, seems to be less an objection to inequality per se and more a general objection to unfairness, in this

---

[8] Martin O'Neill (2013), "Constructing a Contractualist Egalitarianism: Equality After Scanlon," *Journal of Moral Philosophy* 10(4): 439.

[9] Scanlon, *Why Does Inequality Matter?*: 8.

case, the unfairness of economic institutions. We might still object to the same economic institutions, but because they are unfair, and not because they necessarily lead to inequality.[10] So it does not seem to give us a reason to care about intergenerational inequality itself.

At this point it does not appear as though any of Scanlon's person-affecting reasons for preferring equality carry forward into the intergenerational context so if equality is to matter between generations, it will have to be for its own sake.

Telic Egalitarianism

Telic egalitarians hold that inequality between people is in itself bad, regardless of the source of the inequality and even when the individuals in question have no relationship with each other. As Derek Parfit describes the view, "it is in itself bad if there are or ever have been, even in unrelated communities, people who are not equally well off."[11] A telic egalitarian would prefer that inequality between generations (i.e., past, present, and future) be eliminated, regardless of the reason for the existence of that inequality. Given the choice between future people being worse off than or equally as well off as us, telic egalitarians prefer that future people be equally as well off as us because it would be bad if they were worse off. The intergenerational telic egalitarian would think it would be better, at least in one respect, if all generations enjoyed the same level of well-being. So far so good. However, there is also the possibility that future people's quality of life could be substantially *better* than ours, and in this case the telic egalitarian would again prefer that future people not be undeservedly better off than we are. Practically, this

---

[10] It is, after all, possible that something that does not result in inequality might nonetheless be unfair and objectionable for that reason. For example, it would be unfair, but not unequal, if two children were told that if they did some task, they will receive a treat and one does the work and the other does not, but both are given the treat.

[11] Derek Parfit (2000), "Equality or Priority?," in *The Ideal of Equality*, ed. Matthew Clayton and Andrew Williams (Palgrave): 88.

could be achieved by all generations being at the same level as some past generation or the current generation.[12]

There has been a general upwards trajectory in economic development since the Industrial Revolution. In the just sixty years between 1950 and 2010 United States real GDP increased by more than 563%, and the standard of living is expected to double between 2007 and 2100.[13] This means that people are better off economically, but quality of life goes beyond the amount of disposable income people have. It includes improvements in things such as indoor plumbing, motor vehicles, air-conditioning, etc. These innovations not only improve economic performance, but also have a significant effect on other components of well-being such as an individual's ease of living, life prospects, and even expected lifespan. For example, between 1928 and 2005 female life expectancy in Canada rose from 60.6 years to 82.7 and is projected to reach 86 by 2031.[14] Quality of life also includes more subjective considerations such as basic liberties, an increased array of life choices, and opportunities for pursuing important personal projects and goals. Over time these non-economic aspects have also improved. At least in Western countries, for instance, civil rights for women, gays/lesbians, and racial and religious minorities have increased, improving the opportunities and life choices for the members of these groups.

It is evident that we are all already better off than any particular past generation. For all generations to be at the same level as

---

[12] I leave aside the problem of which past generation we choose as the baseline to represent 'past generations' since choosing one would be unavoidably arbitrary and does not change my argument. There is, of course, a third option: that all generations should enjoy the level of future generations. However, since it is impossible to change the level of well-being of people in the past, and next to impossible to raise our own standard of living to what we expect future people to enjoy (wouldn't we have done so already?), I will not consider it.

[13] Robert J. Gordon (2012), "Is US Economic Growth Over? Faltering Innovation Confronts the Six Headwinds," National Bureau for Economic Research, Cambridge, MA.

[14] Statistics Canada, "Life Expectancy," http://www.statcan.gc.ca/pub/82-229-x/2009 001/demo/lif-eng.htm (accessed February 21, 2023).

a past generation (whichever one is selected), we would have to level down. The first step would be to lower the current generation's quality of life, and the reduction could be quite drastic. In order for the current generation to live lives as good as our predecessors', we would have to give up economic purchasing power, most modern conveniences, and some civil liberties. Shlomi Segall believes that opponents of telic egalitarianism use this as an example of one of telic egalitarianism's counterintuitive results and subsequently a reason not to accept the view. However, he suggests that the apparent counterintuitiveness actually springs from two separate issues. The first is that we cannot benefit the dead; following on from that, the second is that it does not make sense to make ourselves worse off for the sake of equality with people from the past who will not be impacted in any way by our decision.[15] He then argues that these two points relate not to whether inequality with the past is bad or not, but to a separate question of whether or not we ought to do anything about it. As a result, in his opinion, they are not objections to telic egalitarianism.

I think Segall is right to separate the two questions, but I don't think it fully solves our problem. With respect to future generations, we *can* impact them and so we need to know whether it might make sense to 'do something about it' and pursue equality with them.[16]

One would be forgiven for being pessimistic about the increase in quality of life continuing in the future, given the predictions of potential catastrophe ubiquitous in the media, especially pertaining to climate change. However, Nicholas Stern estimates that even if very little is done about climate change,

---

[15] Shlomi Segall (2015), "Incas and Aliens: The Truth in Telic Egalitarianism," *Economics and Philosophy* 32.

[16] Also, some people may think equality with the past is irrelevant: since we cannot affect past people's quality of life, we should only look forward. But it *is* possible to equalise with past people (through levelling down), and if we are serious about equality for its own sake, we ought to at least entertain the idea.

global gross domestic product (GDP) is likely to be three times larger by the middle of the century.[17] By all accounts, future generations will be at least economically better off than we are. To achieve equality between us and them, we will need to ensure that future people do not have the opportunity to have better qualities of life than we do—again, we need to level down. One way to do this is for current people to do things like destroy natural resources and technologies they develop, or prevent economic growth. The aim would be to leave future people with fewer goods that they could use to make their standard of living higher than current people.

This 'levelling-down objection' is a well-known criticism of telic egalitarianism and is not unique to the intergenerational context. Some might even consider it a nail in the coffin for telic egalitarianism because it suggests that equality is better, even if it is better for no one. In my view, contractualists should agree that we should not level down for the intrinsic sake of equality, though they do not necessarily need to agree on this for the same reason. Whereas the levelling-down objection is seen by many as a reason to reject the value of intrinsic equality because of its supposedly undesirable consequences, I think contractualists *could* accept that equality has intrinsic value, but deny that this value is a relevant reason to pursue equality between generations (or anyone, for that matter). No one is made better off by levelling down, so the primary reason to do it is the intrinsic value of equality, which is an *impersonal* reason and so excluded from contractualist reasoning. Current and future generations could reasonably reject a principle requiring levelling down on the grounds that it requires a great sacrifice of well-being on their part, yet no one benefits. Furthermore, there is no one who would be burdened by—and therefore object to—an

---

[17] Nicholas Stern (2010), "The Economics of Climate Change," in *Climate Ethics: Essential Readings*, ed. Stephen Gardiner, Simon Caney, Dale Jamieson, and Henry Shue (Oxford University Press).

alternative principle that did not require levelling down and instead allowed inequalities between generations. A telic egalitarian principle would benefit no one but would harm current and/or future generations.

Larry Temkin responds to this line of argument by taking a pluralistic view of egalitarianism wherein there is something *pro tanto* better about equality and that it is only *in one respect* (rather than all things considered) worse for people (generations in this case) to be unequal.[18] But even if we accept this as a response to the levelling-down objection in general, the way in which equality is *pro tanto* better in his view is still impersonal. Temkin's argument is a response to the levelling-down objection, but not a convincing one for a contractualist because an egalitarian needs to provide reasons for choosing intergenerational equality that are based on equality's impact on *persons*.

At this point one might object that the egalitarian claim is not that future generations be as well off as we are, but *at least as well off as we are*. On this view it would be acceptable for them to be better off than we are, but not to be worse off. I certainly feel the pull of the intuition underpinning this claim, but I think that there are still reasons to reject it, primarily because how well off 'we' are is an arbitrary baseline, meaning that the amount owed to future generations is contingent only on how well off the previous generation happens to be and not on what people actually need or how their lives go. Imagine a previous generation that is very poor—its members live barely-worth-living lives. Luckily, a magic wand drops from the sky, allowing them to make the next generation extremely well off such that each member will enjoy a fabulous life. Alternatively, they can ignore the wand and leave the next generation in a state similar to their own. Were they to follow the 'at least as good' principle, they would do nothing wrong by failing to wave the magic wand since they will leave the next generation at least as well off as they

[18] Larry Temkin (2003), "Egalitarianism Defended," *Ethics* 113(4).

are, which is not very well off at all. My claim is that the next generation could reasonably reject a principle allowing the previous generation not to wave the wand. The defence for this claim will come in the next section, but for now it suffices to say that what matters in non-relational circumstances such as non-overlapping generations seems to be not intergenerational comparison but the absolute quality of life people (generations) have the opportunity to enjoy.

In his earlier lectures on equality Scanlon actually identified another personal reason to value equality.[19] *Humanitarianism* says that where the worst-off are very badly off, we have a reason to alleviate their suffering. This reason takes a person's *absolute* level of well-being to be paramount. In the time between those lectures and the publication of his book, several commentators correctly pointed out that *Humanitarianism* is not really a reason for equality at all, and it never made it into the final version of his thoughts on the matter. But although it is not a reason for equality, it does seem *prima facie* plausible that all people, regardless of when they live, could have personal reasons to reject principles that leave them without the means to enjoy decent qualities of life. I think for this reason that the most promising route for a contractualist to follow is to focus on future people's expected *absolute*, rather than *comparative*, quality of life. I now turn to such a task.

Sufficientarianism: Lexical Priority Below the Threshold

There are a variety of different breeds of sufficientarianism, but they generally share two core beliefs: (i) what matters morally is that people live above a certain threshold, free from deprivation (what Paula Casal refers to as the 'positive thesis') and (ii) indifference to

---

[19] T. M. Scanlon (2004), "When Does Equality Matter?," John F. Kennedy School of Government, Harvard University, Cambridge, MA.

distributions above the threshold (Casal's 'negative thesis').[20] The most important element in sufficientarian thought is the claim that there is some threshold of quality of life which justifies treating those above and below it differently.

Some sufficientarians argue that what is most important is for as many people as possible to be above the threshold of sufficiency, however it is defined or drawn.[21] Arneson calls this view 'strict sufficientarianism'[22] but it is also sometimes known as the 'headcount view'.[23] Strict sufficientarians argue that bringing a person to the sufficiency threshold has absolute priority over any welfare gains, not only for those already above the threshold, but also for those so far below it that those gains will not result in them reaching the threshold. Alternatively, 'moderate sufficientarians' give the same lexical priority to those below the threshold as strict sufficientarians do, but they also give priority to those farthest below the threshold rather than to those closest to achieving sufficiency.[24] The consequence of both strict and moderate sufficientarianism is that improving the position of those below the threshold is prioritised over any benefits, no matter how great, to those above it.

To many, including myself, sufficientarianism is *prima facie* intuitively compelling. It does seem of great importance that people live lives that are free from deprivation, and as Casal points out, almost all distributive theories accept at least a minimal version of the positive thesis.[25] However, as some philosophers have noted, despite its initial plausibility, it has some potentially counterintuitive implications. These have been widely discussed,[26] so I will only sketch the three most important.

---

[20] Paula Casal (2007), "Why Sufficiency Is Not Enough," *Ethics* 117(2): 297–98.
[21] Harry Frankfurt (1987), "Equality as a Moral Ideal," *Ethics* 98(1).
[22] Richard Arneson (2005), "Distributive Justice and Basic Capability Equality," in *Capabilities Equality: Basic Issues and Problems*, ed. Alexander Kaufman (Routledge).
[23] Liam Shields (2016), *Just Enough* (Edinburgh University Press).
[24] Roger Crisp (2003), "Equality, Priority, and Compassion," *Ethics* 113 (4).
[25] Casal, "Why Sufficiency Is Not Enough": 299.
[26] For example, in Casal, "Why Sufficiency Is Not Enough," and Richard Arneson, "Distributive Justice and Basic Capability Equality."

Disproportionality. First, assigning lexical priority below the threshold means that both strict and moderate sufficientarianism could require us to use vast quantities of resources and potentially significantly lower some people's (above-threshold) quality of life for the sake of a very small increase for someone below the threshold. It may not seem problematic for priority to be afforded to those who are deprived over those who are not. But consider: "if granting a nontrivial benefit to somebody below the threshold required bringing the rest of humanity down to the threshold, we are required to do it. This requirement is counterintuitive with either a high or low threshold."[27] Neither strict nor moderate sufficientarianism places limits on how much sacrifice/burden can be required of those above the threshold for the sake of those below. A strict or moderate sufficientarian principle could be reasonably rejected by those above the threshold on the grounds that it required a severe and disproportionately high sacrifice relative to the benefits accrued by the worse-off.

Upward Transfers. The objection here is that strict sufficientarian principles could recommend benefiting the better-off by tiny amounts, even if much larger benefits could have been given to the worst-off.[28] Imagine one person is very close to but still slightly below the threshold, and another is far below it. Imagine we have some resources that we can distribute to either person. If we give them to the person close to the threshold, she will be bumped just over it, and if we give them to the other person, they will be significantly benefited but still remain below the threshold. Strict sufficientarianism requires us to prioritise the better-off person since that would result in more people living sufficiently good lives. Since the sufficiency threshold is unavoidably at least somewhat arbitrarily designated, it seems undesirable that it should be given

---

[27] Casal, "Why Sufficiency Is Not Enough": 298–99.
[28] Shields, *Just Enough*: 21; Dale Dorsey (2008), "Towards a Theory of the Basic Minimum," *Politics, Philosophy & Economics* 7(4).

so much importance that the better-off person is automatically prioritized because he happens to be almost at that level to begin with. Indeed, it seems likely that the worse-off person could reasonably reject a principle that distributed in this way, on the grounds of either extra burden (in comparison to the better-off person's claims) or arbitrariness (of using the threshold as a decision-making tool).

Indifference Above the Threshold. The final objection that I want to consider is to the negative thesis specifically. The main criticism of the negative thesis is that it is wrongfully indifferent to distributions above the threshold. Some object to this indifference on the grounds that it allows massive inequalities among those above the threshold, which is problematic, especially the lower the threshold is drawn:

> For example, if the threshold is set at £30,000 or £40,000 annual income and we could help some group who received £50,000 annually or some group who received £900,000 annually, the upper-limit sufficientarian would be indifferent about who gets the help. It seems, however, that we should not be indifferent.[29]

Of course, this problem can be avoided by setting the threshold high enough—at the point where we really are indifferent about distributions, say among billionaires. But if we do that, then sufficientarianism loses its strength as a distributive theory since it is implausible that having 'enough' means having billions of dollars.

But merely saying we should not be indifferent above the threshold is not enough (pun intended). *Why* should we care about above-threshold distributions? Sufficientarianism's indifference above the threshold is due to the lexical priority given to those

---

[29] Shields, *Just Enough*: 24. Not everyone agrees we should be indifferent at high income levels. See James Christensen, Tom Parr, and David V. Axelsen (2022), "Justice for Millionaires?," *Economics & Philosophy* 38(3).

below the threshold, combined with the claim that our distributive obligations are complete once people have reached the threshold. I think these two claims could both be reasonably rejected. Consider the following scenario.

Option 1			Option 2		
Sufficiency = 50	A	B	Sufficiency = 50	A	B
Before Redistribution	49.9	50.1	Before Redistribution	49.9	50.1
After Redistribution	50	50.1	After Redistribution	49.9	60.1

In this scenario, we must choose between two options. In option 1, before redistribution A and B are both very close to the threshold, with A just below and B just above. If this option is chosen, A will receive 0.1 units and B will receive nothing. The parties have the same pre-distribution allocations in option 2, but the benefits will be given to B instead, and these benefits are significantly greater (10 units). Both strict and moderate sufficientarians would prefer option 1 to option 2 because A begins below the threshold and B is above. However, this means that the minuscule benefit that could be bestowed on A, who was already very close to meeting the threshold of sufficiency, would be preferable to the much greater benefit that could be given to B, who was also very close to the threshold (but just a shade above). I think it is plausible that B could reject a principle requiring the tiny benefit be given to A on the grounds of arbitrariness because if the sufficiency level were 49 instead of 50, both A and B would be above it and both strict and moderate sufficientarians would have been indifferent between them. On the other hand, if sufficiency were 51, strict sufficientarianism at least would require the benefits to be bestowed on B since in that case it would be possible to bring B to the level of sufficiency, but not A.

These two scenarios show the heavy lifting that the location of the sufficiency threshold is doing and the moral weight it is given. Changing the threshold by even tiny amounts can radically change to whom we ought to distribute any benefits. While on the surface it seems obviously important that people have (at least) sufficiently good lives, it is hard for me to accept that the threshold should have *such* a crucial moral role when the level at which it is drawn is unavoidably arbitrary and when both parties had almost identical initial levels of well-being.

Furthermore, it is not at all clear to me that our ethical duties are totally fulfilled once all people are sufficiently well off. Imagine your sufficiently well-off neighbour came to you and asked you to help her by collecting her mail for a week. Would you reply: "No, sorry, you are already sufficiently well off, so I have no duties to you to improve your well-being by helping you"? I hope not! This is especially true when helping her would require little to no sacrifice on your part. You may decline to help for other reasons, like you are away yourself, or you broke your leg and it would be significantly burdensome to go over to her house to collect the mail, but not simply because she is already sufficiently well off. If I am able to improve someone's quality of life at no or very little cost to myself, there seems to be no reason I should not do so. It could be objected that sufficientarianism does not preclude helping people who are above the sufficiency threshold, simply that it is not morally required. However, in contractualist terms, the other person would have a reason to want to be benefited, I have no reason not to benefit, so there is no one who could reasonably reject a principle requiring me to benefit. It would therefore be morally obligatory that I make the other person better off. Particularly when parties enjoy levels of well-being above the threshold of sufficiency, this reason-based thinking is not captured by the types of sufficientarianism I described above.

Although I have argued that there are contractualist and non-contractualist objections to certain elements of strict and moderate sufficientarianism, I still think the importance of people having good enough lives, free from deprivation, has considerable intuitive force. The remainder of this chapter develops what I will call *reason-balanced sufficientarianism* to capture this intuition without (i) requiring disproportionately high burdens on those above the threshold for the sake of small gains to those below it; (ii) prioritising the best-off rather than the worst-off in order to bring as many people as possible above the threshold; (iii) according lexical priority to the threshold; (iv) being indifferent to the distribution of benefits above the threshold.

Reason-Balanced Sufficiency

Let's start by sketching out the basics of what I call 'reason-balanced sufficiency' and why contractualists should endorse it as a distributive theory.

It is important to be aware of two important points. First, finding principles no one can reasonably reject requires balancing the reasons different parties have, and the strength of these reasons can change depending on the circumstances. Second, we need to understand what role the sufficiency threshold should play in light of these different circumstances. How do we accomplish these tasks?

Contractualism allows for variation in what is right and wrong by applying a fixed set of moral principles to varying circumstances because "in different social conditions people will have different generic reasons for rejecting proposed principles" (340). This means that an action that would be wrong in one context might be unobjectionable in another. To put it another way, contractualist reasoning is based on what people have reason to want, and what they have reason to want is based on the conditions in which they are placed. Scanlon even argues that even if that were not the case and the strength of reasons were fixed, thresholds for reasonable rejection would not make sense:

> [T]he idea might be that there is a threshold of reasonable rejection: a level of cost such that it is reasonable to reject any principle that would lead to one's suffering a cost that great, and reasonable to do this no matter what objections others might have to alternative principles. It does not seem to me that there is such a threshold. (196)

He illustrates this point by using examples of what he thinks contractualism would require us to do to help people in two different situations: those who are in dire need and those who are not. Beginning with the first, he defines those in 'dire need' as people whose lives are immediately threatened, who are starving, who are in great pain, or who are living in conditions of bare subsistence. He says that in these cases, the following principle would be non-rejectable:

> *Rescue Principle*: When you can prevent something very bad from happening, or alleviate someone's dire plight by making only a slight or moderate sacrifice, you must do so. (224)

In this case the person in dire need's reason for requiring assistance is stronger than the reason the better-off person has to avoid making small or moderate sacrifices, meaning *Rescue* cannot be reasonably rejected. That we have an obligation to assist those facing extreme hardships (or to prevent those hardships from befalling them in the first instance) when it requires only a small or moderate sacrifice should be, I think, relatively uncontroversial. But this is not necessarily the full extent of our obligations, just their starting point: the 'dire straits' end of the spectrum, if you will. At this end, at a minimum, a moderate sacrifice from the rescuer is required, but what about the other end, when others are not in great need?

Imagine you have some information that would help another person. This person is already well off, but the information would make her even better off because it would save her time and effort, say, in the course of pursuing a project. Scanlon argues:

> [I]t would surely be wrong of [you] to fail (simply out of indifference) to give her this information when there is no compelling reason not to do so. It would be unreasonable to reject a principle requiring us to help others in this way (even when they are not in desperate need), since such a principle would involve no significant sacrifice on our part. (224)

This *Helpfulness* principle requires us to help others when we can do so at little to no cost. It is not merely optional or a 'nice thing to do', but morally required, and it would be wrong not to. In this case, the sacrifice required in order to provide additional benefits to someone who is not in serious need is much lower.

In both *Rescue* and *Helpfulness*, the person being helped has a reason to want help/benefits, but the strength of that reason differs based on their circumstances—in our example, their level of need. Crucially, even in *Rescue*, the reasons the person in need has do not *automatically* take priority over any reasons the rescuer might have; because the person in need's reasons are very weighty, they will outweigh many or even most of the rescuer's reasons, but there is still a chance that the rescuer might have some stronger reason not to rescue.

The strength of reasons can change according to circumstance, and my claim is that a person's proximity to the sufficiency threshold is a circumstance that changes the strength of their reason to demand assistance. Liam Shields agrees, calling this the 'shift thesis':

> Once a person has had enough sleep or enough petrol for his or her car, we do not think that there are no further benefits to securing more sleep or petrol, as the [negative thesis] would. Instead, we think that once enough petrol or sleep is secured, our reasons to put more petrol in our cars or to spend more time

asleep are changed. A countervailing reason can more easily outweigh our reasons to get more than enough of some good than it can outweigh our reasons to secure just enough of that good. Sufficiency thresholds characterised as a shift or change in our reasons can explain why.[30]

Shields believes that the shift thesis explains why we should not adopt the negative thesis and be indifferent to distributions above the threshold, but I think the threshold changes reasons below the threshold too, explaining why we should not always give absolute priority below the threshold either.

We have already seen that there are certain cases in which, intuitively, it seems not necessarily to be required to prioritize bringing people to the sufficiency threshold (though admittedly some sufficientarians would disagree). These included instances in which it would take a disproportionately high quantity of resources in order to do so, or when we should instead help people who are much worse off but have no hope of reaching sufficiency. However, there are also likely to be cases in which it *would* clearly seem to be required. If, for example, A were at 45 and B were at 500 (sufficiency is again 50), and B could give up 5 units in order to bring A up to 50, it would seem to be required of him that he do so. Let us flesh out why sufficiency seems to be crucial in some cases but not in others.

When a sufficientarian gives lexical priority to the sufficiency threshold, they are also giving absolute weight to the reason to want to secure sufficiency. This means that the reason for wanting to achieve sufficiency will outweigh any other reasons that may exist (e.g., making worse-off people better off, benefiting more people, considerations of proportionality, etc.). In this way the sufficiency threshold acts as a trump and any person who has this reason (by virtue of being below the threshold) would be able to reject any principle that does not prioritise it over all other reasons.

---

[30] Shields, *Just Enough*: 27.

But the inherently comparative nature of contractualism precludes allowing certain reasons to always outweigh others. Rather than assigning a reason absolute priority over all other reasons, all reasons must be balanced against each other, including the reason to want to reach the sufficiency threshold. Even the reason to want to save your own life—presumably as good a candidate for a trumping reason as any—Scanlon argues does not always outweigh other reasons:

> [I]t does not seem that the fact that a principle would forbid one to do something that was necessary in order to save one's life *always* makes it reasonable to reject that principle. (196, my emphasis)

This is because the reasonableness of rejection will also depend on the costs imposed on others and how those costs are distributed. For example, the fact that a principle would forbid you from stealing a kidney from someone else in order to save your life with a transplant does not mean that it is reasonable for you to reject the principle.

I believe our intuitions about the cases earlier support the idea that while we should give sufficiency a significant degree of weight, we must still balance it against other reasons. When sufficiency is given high importance, it can outweigh many considerations, but not *every* other consideration. This would track the intuition that we ought not always spend considerable resources to prioritize bringing one person above the threshold instead of helping another much worse-off person who will nonetheless remain below it. It is also consistent with the belief that a very well-off person ought to make a certain (though proportionate) sacrifice in order to help bring another person above the threshold.

All people have a reason to want to live at least decent lives with enough food, health, and physical security (among other things) to be able to pursue their individual goals and projects that are important to them. A person at the sufficiency level has the opportunity to meet and continue to securely meet all of their basic human needs and has the capacity to be an autonomous, rational agent capable of performing the tasks expected of fully functioning members of society.

The reason to want to have the opportunity for a sufficiently good life is actually subsidiary to the more basic reason to want to maximize one's quality of life. Every person, perhaps barring some ascetics, has a reason to want to improve his or her quality of life, whatever their current level may be.[31] The weightiness of this reason strengthens as the person's quality of life goes down: a person very far below sufficiency will have an extremely strong reason for wanting a better quality of life, whereas a person at sufficiency has a weaker reason, and a person well beyond it has a much weaker reason still. As a result, people who do not yet have sufficiently good lives have a much stronger reason to demand assistance from others than those people who do. On my account, the sufficiency threshold does not play a determinative role (where those below get assistance and those above don't), but rather is a signpost to guide us in comparing the strength of different people's reasons for demanding assistance from others.

At this point it may appear as though I am advocating a form of prioritarianism. According to prioritarians, benefits matter more the worse off someone is.[32] The difference between prioritarianism and sufficientarianism is that for prioritarians there is no specific absolute amount of well-being for which they are aiming. Rather, if there are benefits to be bestowed, they ought to be given to the worst-off, even if the worst-off person is well above sufficiency. For example, if sufficiency is understood to be 50 units, and A has 300 units and B has 500 units, any additional units available to

---

[31] If reasons are universal, as Scanlon claims, then even ascetics also have this reason, but it is not a motivating reason in their life.
[32] Parfit, "Equality or Priority?"

be distributed ought, according to prioritarianism, to be given to A. One difference between prioritarianism and the view that I am defending is that it is not necessarily the case that these benefits always ought to be given to A. Since A is well above sufficiency, her claim to additional resources is weak, although still somewhat stronger than B's. In this case other reasons could come into play as a way of arbitrating between the two parties' claims for the additional units, desert perhaps. Additionally, a person might object to the burden placed on the more advantaged party (B), and it might be reasonable for people to reject the kinds of policies needed to promote the condition of the least advantaged. If the additional units are redistributed from B to A, who is already well above the sufficiency level, B could object that it was unfair since (for example) he worked hard to create those units. A would have to have very strong reasons to demand more since her quality of life is already far above sufficiency.

Back to the Future

What I have called 'reason-balanced sufficiency' means that if we were considering a principle that would leave future people without the opportunity to lead sufficiently good lives, their reason(s) to object to it would be very strong and would require at least an equally strong reason from current people to avoid being rejected. This means that in the absence of any such countervailing reasons, we are required to provide enough resources to give future people the opportunity to enjoy at least sufficiently good lives.[33] Once future generations have enough resources to do so, their reasons for wanting to have the opportunity to improve their quality of

---

[33] I will discuss later in this section what these sorts of equally strong, countervailing reasons could be.

life become weaker and more easily outweighed by the sacrifices needed from the current generation to provide it.

This means that in most cases, a principle requiring us to leave future generations with at least enough resources to give them the opportunity to secure decent lives could not be reasonably rejected. Here is such a principle:

> *Sufficient Resources*: The current generation must leave future generations with enough resources to have the opportunity to enjoy sufficiently good lives, unless doing so would be disproportionately burdensome.

Obviously the most important point to clarify is what is meant by 'disproportionately burdensome', so let's tease this out.

The first step is to determine the strength of reasons held by current and future people, assuming for now that the former already have sufficiently good lives themselves. As I said earlier, in general, the reasons for assistance held by those below the sufficiency threshold are very strong but do not have lexical priority over all other reasons. If they would not otherwise have the opportunity to live sufficiently good lives, future people have a stronger reason to demand benefits than already sufficiently well-off current people do. But benefits are not the whole story, and we must also look at any potential burdens for current people, either through sacrificing/giving up things they already have or through refraining from using resources to further improve their own lives. If the burdens faced by current people above the threshold are sufficiently great relative to the benefits future people stand to gain, the people above the threshold may not be required to make that sacrifice.

Let's see how this works in a straightforward case. In many cases it will be possible to provide sufficiency for future people through only a moderate sacrifice from current people. Perhaps we would have to save more oil than we would like, and therefore need to take public transportation more often than private cars, which is somewhat inconvenient. Let's further stipulate that doing so will make the difference between future people having insufficient versus sufficiently good lives. In this type of case, current people would not have grounds for failing to provide future people with the opportunity for sufficiency because their reason for wanting to lead even better lives (by using private cars and avoiding the inconvenience of public transit) are substantially weaker than the very strong reason future people have to want the opportunity for at least sufficiently good lives.

Although *Sufficient Resources* leaves open the possibility that the current generation might not always be required to provide sufficiency for the future, I see only two main cases where this proviso would kick in. The first is the unfortunate situation where current people would have to sacrifice their own sufficiency in order to provide future people with enough resources to secure theirs. In this case we would have two conflicting reasons for wanting sufficiency which are of equal weight. In these cases I think it would be permissible for current people to use the resources necessary to ensure their own sufficiency even if that means future generations will be unable to do so themselves. This is because, unlike positions like Peter Singer's,[34] contractualism does not require us always to be completely impartial. Principles that forbid us from giving our own interests any extra weight could be reasonably rejected because they are "intolerably intrusive" and "impartial reasoning . . . leads to the conclusion that we are not required to be impartial in each actual decision we make" because everyone has a generic reason not to want to be bound by a strict requirement never to give special weight to one's own interests (225). It could be objected that since there are so many more future people than current people, the former's interests should be aggregated and would therefore take on a greater weight. However, as we know, aggregating in this way is excluded from the contractualist way of thinking (229–41).

---

[34] Peter Singer (2011), *Practical Ethics*, 3rd ed. (Cambridge University Press).

The second case is where a large sacrifice by current people was required for the sake of a very small benefit to future people. One of the objections levelled against strict sufficientarianism was that it fetishized the threshold such that huge sacrifices could be required of an above-threshold person A for the sake of a very small increase to a just-barely-below-threshold person B that pushed her just to the threshold. Following *Sufficient Resources*, A could argue that the burdens to her are disproportionately high relative to the very small increase to A. Since we are not giving lexical priority to the threshold, the fact that, say, 0.1 units of benefit to B would push her to the threshold is not a decisive reason to oblige A to give up, say 950 units. Since reasons held by those below the threshold (in this example, B) are given a lot of weight, the potential burden (or sacrificed benefit) for A would have to be quite high in order to outweigh B's reasons. What is notable is that the principle is open to this possibility in a way that standard forms of sufficientarianism are not.

What If We Can't Provide Enough?

I just argued that when current generations cannot ensure that future people will be sufficiently well off without disproportionate burden, they are not required to do so. However, this account remains incomplete. Does it mean that in a situation where we cannot provide sufficiency without incurring disproportionate burdens, our obligations to provide for the future are no more? Can we then use as many resources as we wish? Surely not. Even if we cannot leave enough, that should not mean we have no obligations at all. As we've seen, we are allowed to give some extra weight to our own interests, which is why we are allowed to prioritize our own sufficiency over that of future generations when only one can be ensured. However, even if we are unable to provide sufficiency to the next generation(s), we must still take their interests into account when deciding what to do. As it stands, the principle of *Sufficient Resources* doesn't give us any guidance about our obligations when the sacrifices the current generation must make in order to provide sufficiency are considered severe or disproportionate.

Imagine that the current generation decides (permissibly) to use the resources at their disposal to achieve sufficiency for themselves. It may be the case that in doing so they have exhausted all of the resources available. However, if there are still some resources left (albeit not enough to guarantee sufficiency for subsequent generations), what is the current generation permitted to do with them? They are required to save them for the next generation rather than using them for improving their own well-being above sufficiency levels.

It may seem like I am trying to slip a 'headcount' view of sufficientarianism in through the back door, but this is not the case. Rather, it is because once the current generation is sufficiently well off, it is no longer a severe sacrifice to save for the future. Once the current generation has achieved a decent quality of life, it would be at most a moderate sacrifice to ensure that future people are better off than they would be if the current generation used the leftover resources for themselves. The current generation's reason for wanting to increase their quality of life beyond sufficiency is much weaker than future generations' reason to want to increase their future quality of life, given that the latter will be below sufficiency no matter what. Future generations could reasonably object that by increasing our life prospects beyond sufficiency by failing to conserve anything for future people, we have shown a complete disregard for their interests. In fact, I would argue that the current generation even has a duty to try to achieve sufficiency for themselves as efficiently as possible. That is, they ought to try to achieve sufficiency in a way that uses as few resources as they can in order to leave the next generations as close to sufficiency as possible. This means we ought to actively search for ways (e.g., new technologies) to use fewer resources to achieve sufficiency.

This discussion suggests that when it is not possible to satisfy *Sufficient Resources*, the following principle applies:

> *Insufficient Resources*: When the current generation is not able to provide future generations with the opportunity to live sufficiently good lives without sacrificing sufficiency themselves, the current generation is permitted to prioritize their own sufficiency. Once the current generation has achieved sufficiency, they must try to leave future generations as well off as possible.

Is it Enough to Leave Enough?

I have claimed that future people could not reject the principles above since their reason for wanting sufficiently good lives is given a very high weight, higher than current people's reasons for wanting better than sufficiently good lives themselves. But could they reject *Sufficient Resources* on the grounds that we ought to be doing *more* than just leaving them with enough? Although leaving future generations with enough resources for sufficiency will usually be the minimum required of current generations, in some cases it will not exhaust our moral obligations. As I argued earlier, when improving someone else's (already adequate) quality of life could be done with only minimal sacrifice, it is morally required, analogously to Scanlon's *Helpfulness* principle. I believe the same is true in the case of intergenerational distribution. If it is possible to leave future generations with even more than the resources required for the opportunity to live sufficiently good lives, at minimal cost to the current generation, it ought to be done. This is because it would be impossible for the current generation to justify *not* doing so. Since it is done at minimal cost, there is no reason for current people to reject a principle that required it. In my view, the following principle could not be reasonably rejected:

Additional Resources: The current generation is required to leave resources to give future generations the opportunity to enjoy more than sufficiently good lives if it would require minimal or no sacrifice.

My claim is that in most cases our minimum obligation is to provide future generations with the opportunity to lead sufficiently good lives. However, when doing so would cause the current generation a disproportionately high burden, such as sacrificing sufficiency for themselves, or when the benefits to the future are very small relative to the sacrifice required, we are permitted to give our own interests additional weight and use the resources we need in order to ensure sufficiency for ourselves. In addition to the minimum, it is required to do more still when it would take no or minimal sacrifice on our part. Beyond that, any additional benefits we choose to leave for them are supererogatory.

My conclusion is that together the principles I have outlined accommodate the strong intuition that it is very important that people have the opportunity to live sufficiently good lives in a way that avoids the objections to strict and moderate sufficientarian I made earlier:

Disproportionality. The principle of *Sufficient Resources* precludes disproportionate burdens being required for the sake of small gains to those below (or indeed above) the threshold.

Upward Transfers. The threshold acts as a signpost to help us determine a person's strength of reasons. Those closest to the threshold will have weaker reasons to demand assistance relative to those further away from it. Therefore, the worst-off under the threshold will have very strong reasons to demand extra assistance and will, in most (but not all) cases, be prioritized.

Indifference Above the Threshold. The *Additional Resources* principle holds that there are moral requirements to assist those above the threshold if the burden incurred by doing so are at most minimal.

For the purposes of this chapter I have assumed that the size of the next generation was fixed and knowable. However, population size is of course not fixed and we have a significant amount of control over how big the next few generations will be. The size of the next generations will affect how the principles I have laid out above will be applied. If the next generation is very large, they will require more resources in order to achieve sufficiently good lives, possibly requiring a greater sacrifice from us. Whether this sacrifice is still considered moderate or whether it becomes severe will also affect which principle of resource distribution applies— i.e., *Sufficient Resources* or *Insufficient Resources*. Likewise, if the next generation is very small, we may be required to do more for them because it would only require a minor sacrifice from us and *Additional Resources* may be the principle that applies. At the limit, if there is no next generation, of course none of the principles in this chapter will kick in and we will be permitted to do whatever we wish with the resources that we have. For this reason, I will discuss what population sizes would be permitted under the contractualist framework in Chapter 5. But next, I turn to applying the same 'reason-balanced sufficiency' theory to the problem of individual procreative decisions.

4
Permissible Procreation

In the last chapter I argued that we need to balance a future person's reason for wanting the opportunity for a sufficiently good life against the reasons current people may have not to provide it. This chapter uses the same method to explore when it is permissible and impermissible for individual people to procreate.

Some people might resist applying the same considerations to procreation as we did to a much less personal issue like natural resources. The argument could be that there is something special about procreation that simply does not exist when we are discussing the conservation of physical/natural resources. For one thing, when we use personal resources (gametes), we create a new person with whom we have a special relationship and possibly special obligations. Another difference is that the natures of the bads that the future person/people might experience are different in kind. Living in poverty or with a polluted environment is different in kind from having a painful disease or disability. Finally, the nature of the sacrifices made by the duty bearer (current people in our case) is different—abstaining from having children (for example) is different from abstaining from consuming natural resources.

However, despite the fact that procreation may seem different at first, I believe these differences are more relevant to the *reasons* people use to justify/reject principles than to the principles themselves. Individuals face relevantly similar considerations when deliberating about resources as they do when considering whether or not to have a child. On one hand, we must think about the quality of life of others—either future generations writ large, or a particular child that will be brought into the world—and on the other hand, we consider the sacrifices current people have to bear in order to secure various qualities of life for future people (either in general, or the particular future person that they have created). At a fundamental level, both issues contribute to or detract from the well-being enjoyed by future people and are not so very different, and the same reasoning can apply to both.

When Is It Permissible to Procreate?

In order to determine when it is permissible to procreate, we need to consider various principles that could govern procreation.

Whenever You Want

Let's start with the most permissive.

Free Procreation: It is permissible to procreate whenever one wishes to do so.[1]

Free Procreation permits parents to procreate whenever they want, even if they know that the child will have a very bad, or even less-than-worth living, life.

It is presumably uncontroversial that a person could reasonably reject a principle that left them with a life that is less than worth living. Of course, how often less-than-worth-living lives come about depends on what we take quality of life to be. However, Melinda Roberts suggests what I think is a plausible definition: when a life is, on balance, so full of pain and lacking in well-being that the person would be better off never having existed at all, we may say that their

---

[1] I assume that other relevant considerations are in place—such as a willing partner, access to legally acquired funds for in vitro fertilization, etc. These considerations are important and lacking them could provide other reasons for rejecting the principle; however, it is the conditions of the resulting child that I wish to focus on, and so I assume these other factors to be in order.

life is not worth living.[2] The reasons for rejecting such a life are obvious: pain and misery so extreme that they outweigh any positive aspects in the person's life. It seems clear to me that there would be good reasons for a person born into these conditions to reject any principle, including *Free Procreation*, that permitted the intentional or foreseeable creation of a child who will have a life that is not worth living.[3] Any alternative principle that forbade such acts of creation could not be reasonably rejected since the only potential grounds for rejection (the desire of the parent to create the child) could surely be outweighed by the extreme suffering that would be inflicted.

Creating the Best Possible Child

What about the other end of the spectrum of restrictiveness? Here I will consider what Julian Savulescu calls 'procreative beneficence'. Procreative beneficence holds that a person ought to create the child (out of the options available to them) who is expected to have the best possible life.[4] By 'best possible', Savulescu means two things. First, he means that parents ought (where possible) to choose to bear children who will be as free of disease or disability as possible. Assuming pre-implantation genetic testing is done, if a parent must choose between implanting an embryo with physical disabilities and implanting one without any disabilities, they

---

[2] Melinda A. Roberts (1998), *Child Versus Childmaker: Future Persons and Present Duties in Ethics and the Law* (Rowman & Littlefield): 135.

[3] Throughout this chapter I will assume that the problems the children have are imposed intentionally, or at least that they should have reasonably ought to have been foreseen, rather than occurring purely by chance or accident. This is because it does not seem plausible to me that an outcome could be wrong without intention or negligence. For example, if a couple ends up creating a child with a very bad life through no fault of their own and without negligence, it might be bad that the child was created, but one could not say that the parents acted wrongly.

[4] Julian Savulescu (2001), "Procreative Beneficence: Why We Should Select the Best Children," *Bioethics* 15(5–6): 415.

ought to choose the latter. The second way a child's life can go 'best' is by having certain positive traits (like intelligence or physical attractiveness) and not having certain other negative traits (such as a predisposition to violent outbursts or a very poor memory) that will, respectively, help or hinder his or her chances of success in life. Like with disability and disease, Savulescu argues that wherever possible, parents ought to choose the child who will have the best combination of these non-disease characteristics, however one determines what the best combination is.

Is procreative beneficence reasonably rejectable? The principle can be stated as:

> *Procreative Beneficence*: Wherever possible, a prospective parent P must create the child C with the best possible chance in life by selecting a child without disease or disability genes and with as many other positive traits as possible.

At first it would not seem like C would have any reason to reject the principle. If it is followed, C will have as healthy a body and as many positive behaviour and personality traits as was possible for P to create. If C has a good life—and, indeed, not just the best life *he* could have had, but the best life that P could have created—there does not seem to be any reason for him to reject *Procreative Beneficence*. But this is too quick.

While *Procreative Beneficence* tells us what to do when faced with a choice between creating two different children, it doesn't provide any guidance on the permissibility of creating even the best child when that child will have a very bad life. *Procreative Beneficence* could be consistent with the creation of a very badly-off child if that child is still the best possible child P could create. If a child is very badly off, it does not improve his lot to know that he is P's best possible child. *Procreative Beneficence* is focused on comparative goodness of outcomes and ignores the absolute level of quality of life lived by the resultant child. This means that a child who is born with a very bad (but best possible for P to create) life could reasonably reject *Procreative Beneficence* because of their very low quality of life.

The parents may also have reason to reject this principle. On the surface it seems intuitively plausible that when faced with the choice, P would have good reason to create the best possible child, or at least would have no good reason not to. However, this is only true in certain circumstances. Let us first imagine that the selection of C is being done through choosing a particular embryo to implant as part of the process of in vitro fertilization (IVF) and subsequent pre-implantation genetic diagnosis. If P has already gone through the process and is faced with a choice of embryos and information about the positive and negative traits of each, then I agree that there doesn't seem to be any good reason for P not to choose the best possible embryo. In that straightforward case contractualism would likely support a principle that required procreative beneficence (although there might still be social reasons to object to it).

However, what if P has not already started the process of IVF treatments? *Procreative Beneficence* specifies that 'wherever possible' P ought to create the best possible C. Imagine a case in which, regardless of how, when, or with whom P conceives, the resulting child is guaranteed to have a reasonably good life. If P has the financial means to go through IVF treatments, then it is *possible* for her to select the best C in this manner and *Procreative Beneficence* would require her to do so despite the fact that it would be very demanding physically and otherwise, including financially. Inmaculada de Melo-Martín has detailed these burdens, especially for women, which Savulescu completely overlooks.[5] P would have reason to object to a principle requiring her to go through IVF on the grounds that it forced her to undergo expensive, invasive, and painful medical procedures which she does not want to endure.

---

[5] Inmaculada de Melo-Martín (2004), "On Our Obligation to Select the Best Children: A Reply to Savulescu," *Bioethics* 18(1).

Considering that the child C will be at least adequately well off regardless,[6] it does not seem reasonable to require that P undertake this burden.

This suggests that a blanket principle like *Procreative Beneficence* could be reasonably rejected. It may be true that in some circumstances P is required to create the best possible child, but not at any cost—more on this later. Given that we have also ruled out total procreative liberty, we need to look for something in between these extremes.

A Sufficiency Threshold?

One possible location of the 'in-between' point we are looking for might be what Weinberg calls 'birthright principles' (but which she does not endorse), which claim that there is some minima to which children are entitled and below which procreation is morally impermissible and above which it is permissible.[7]

Birthright principles could also be characterized as sufficientarian—if a prospective parent knew that the child would not have a sufficiently good life (i.e., a life above the minima), he or she ought not to create the child. While it would be morally impermissible to create children below the sufficiency threshold (who nonetheless have lives well worth living), it would presumably not be morally required to maximize expected life prospects above the threshold.

---

[6] I address what to do when C is not already assured of an adequately good life later in the chapter.

[7] Rivka Weinberg (2015), *The Risk of a Lifetime* (Oxford University Press): 191–92. For examples of such a view, she directs readers to: Joel Feinberg (1986), "Wrongful Life and the Counterfactual Element in Harming," *Social Philosophy and Policy* 4; Bonnie Steinbock (1986), "The Logical Case for Wrongful Life," *Hastings Center Report* 16; Jonathan Glover (2006), *Choosing Children: Genes, Disability, and Design* (Oxford University Press). See also Frances Kamm (1992), *Creation and Abortion: A Study in Moral and Legal Philosophy* (Oxford University Press).

While I agree that parents should strive to create children with (at least) good enough lives, I do not think a contractualist can support a specific threshold at which point it is always permissible or impermissible to create above or below, respectively. As we saw in the last chapter, this is because an absolute sufficiency threshold level does not take into account the different reasons (and their relative strengths) parents in different circumstances will have and the balance that must be struck between them and what children are entitled to.

To illustrate, imagine two women, Sally and Theresa. Both women, were they to conceive, could only create a child with a life just below the sufficiency threshold, wherever it is drawn. Sally already has three children, whereas Theresa has none. The burden to Sally in not having another child would be significantly less than the burden Theresa would face. Sally already has the benefit of having children, and the personal fulfilment and joy that come along with that. Having an additional child would provide some added benefit to her life, but not as much as if it were her first child. Theresa, however, would benefit significantly from having a child since if she were not permitted to do, she would be unable to enjoy the pleasures of creating and rearing a biological child. Both women in this case have a reason to want to have a child, but given their different circumstances, Theresa's reason is much stronger.[8] Balanced against the reasons any child would have not to want to be born below the sufficiency threshold, it is possible that Sally's reason to want an additional child would not outweigh the child's reasons to want sufficiency, whereas Theresa's stronger reason could. In this case, at least, it could be wrong for Sally to have a child but not for

---

[8] Another scenario could be one in which Sally could have a child above the threshold but is choosing not to for some reason, whereas the only way Theresa can have a child is if the child is just below the threshold. Whatever sacrifices Sally would need to make to avoid having a below-threshold child would be less burdensome than those that Theresa has to make (abstaining from conception altogether).

Theresa to do so, despite the fact that the resulting child in both cases will live a life just below sufficiency.

The second reason an absolute sufficiency threshold is insufficient on its own is that it gives no guidance to procreation above the threshold. A sufficientarian may not see that as a problem: what matters is that children are above sufficiency. However, it does not seem correct to me that, for instance, in the case of a parent choosing between two embryos, both of which will be sufficiently well off no matter what, it is entirely supererogatory to choose the child who is expected to have a higher quality of life when there are no reasons at all to support the selection of a child with a lower expected quality of life. A sufficientarian view that includes the negative thesis would give no consideration to the reasons a child would have to want as high a quality of life as possible when balanced against the reasons (or lack thereof in this case) that the parent has not to provide it.

I suggest, instead, that there is no absolute threshold of a prospective child's quality of life at which point parents can or cannot procreate. Such a threshold above/below which it is always permissible/impermissible to procreate would not reflect the variability in reasons and circumstances that contractualism is designed to capture.

Contractualist Procreative Principles

The reason to reject *Free Creation* had to do with the negative impacts on the child's quality of life, and the reason to reject *Procreative Beneficence* was that it demanded too much of the prospective parents. Both prospective children and parents have important interests in the procreative process, and both need to be taken into account.

In her book *The Risk of a Lifetime*, Rivka Weinberg offers a Rawlsian contractualist method in which we reason behind the veil of ignorance to determine what procreative principles we would be willing to accept, given that they will govern both our own creation and our right to procreate ourselves. Weinberg argues that reasoning in this way would lead us to a principle of *'Procreative Balance'* where "procreation is permissible when the risk you impose as a procreator on your children would not be irrational for you to accept as a condition of your own birth (assuming that you will exist), in exchange for the permission to procreate under these risk conditions."[9] The principle is tempered by the 'Motivation Restriction', which holds that "procreation must be motivated by the desire and intention to raise, love, and nurture one's own child once it is born."[10]

The consequences of the principles I will argue for in what follows are not too dissimilar to Weinberg's. This is perhaps not completely surprising considering she is also working from a contractualist foundation, albeit of a different vintage. There are some important differences, however. First, the issue of parental motivation plays a different role in my account than it does in hers. For Weinberg, even if a particular procreative choice were allowed according to *Procreative Balance*, if the motivation for procreation is not to raise and nurture your own child, it is impermissible. This means, for example, that a man who donates sperm to a lesbian couple allowing them to have a happy and much-loved child would be acting wrongly since he is not intending to raise and nurture the child himself. On my account, motivation matters, but only insofar as it generates reasons to justify principles to others, in particular to the child(ren) being created. Motivations/reasons for procreation can be broader than merely 'wanting to have and nurture a child'; they just need to be personal and justifiable to the child. The sperm donor can justify his actions to the child on the grounds that he wanted to help his friends have a happy, healthy child. Second,

---

[9] Weinberg, *The Risk of a Lifetime*: 179.
[10] Ibid., 176.

Weinberg's theory is concerned with *intra*personal balancing—that is, what would I be willing to accept about my own creation in exchange for being able to procreate myself? My account is one of *inter*personal balancing, where we balance the interests and reasons of the person being created with those of the person doing the creating. Finally, Weinberg puts risk into the equation from the get-go, whereas at this point I am assuming we know what the consequences of our actions will be. I will talk about risk later, in Chapter 6.

Bad Lives

At one end of the spectrum of possible qualities of life are those with lives that are worth living, but nonetheless bad because they are below the sufficiency threshold. What does it mean to have a bad life? There are any number of things that make life worth living and contribute to a person's quality of life. These can include measurable things like economic and financial security or physical health and the absence of disease, or less tangible goods like strong personal relationships or engagement with your community. A life becomes worth living when, on balance, the good aspects of a person's life outweigh the bad. But there is a gradient of lives above this level and a person could have a life that only barely met this criterion, or one that vastly exceeded it. Some things that could make a life bad include, but are not limited to, having inadequate nutrition or shelter, painful diseases or disabilities, involuntary social isolation, and a lack of loving relationships.

Do we have an obligation not to create a child with a bad life? Recall the *Rescue* principle:

> *Rescue*: When you can prevent something very bad from happening, or alleviate someone's dire plight by making only a slight or moderate sacrifice, you must do so. (224)

We can't relieve someone's plight through creating them,[11] but we can prevent something very bad from happening. Creating a person with a bad life would undoubtedly constitute an instance of causing something very bad to happen, and preventing the creation of a person with a very bad life would be an instance of preventing something very bad from happening. Some might doubt this. By definition, a bad life is worth living, so how could it be bad? On a more impersonal level, it is bad for there to be people with insufficiently good lives. This is part of the reason we try to help people who live in poverty, for example. On a personal level, a person who has a bad life has reason to reject a principle that led to their circumstances. Remember that contractualism's response to the non-identity problem means that a person can still reasonably reject a principle even if that principle led to their existence. This is because existence is seen as a mechanism or precondition for having benefits, not a benefit itself.

A child intentionally created with a bad life has reason to reject a principle that allowed it, because of the negative aspects of their life that make it bad, like a serious disease. At a minimum, therefore, contractualism would endorse the following principle:

> *Bad Lives*: It is impermissible to create a child who will have an insufficiently good life when it would take only a small or moderate sacrifice for the parent(s) to prevent it.[12]

---

[11] I stipulated earlier that the 'conditions' of possible people were not relevant. Thus, the potential (and implausible in my view) objection that non-existence is so bad that creating a person could relieve those possible people of it is put aside.

[12] It should be noted that to say that a parent was wrong to cause a child to exist knowing he would be below the threshold is not to discount the value of the child's life. It would, for example, be wrong for a parent to intentionally and avoidably create a child with no legs. However, this does not mean once the child is born that their life is worth less than that of a normally abled child. It also does not mean that the world is somehow worse because of the existence of this child. Rather, it is simply a moral evaluation of the parents' actions that claims that the parents acted wrongly in creating a child with that disability.

'Preventing it' may mean preventing any child from being born (if any child the parents have will have an insufficiently good life) or having a different child who will have a sufficiently good life.

Some examples will help illustrate how this principle might require small or moderate sacrifices from prospective parents. Spina bifida is a birth defect that occurs when the spinal column does not close completely around the spinal cord. The most common form of the condition can cause physical disabilities such as leg paralysis, bladder and bowel incontinence, scoliosis, and frequent infections. Neurological symptoms are often also present including hydrocephalus, brain damage, poor memory, and problem-solving skills, and individuals with the condition generally lag far behind their peers in mathematics and reading skills. As a result of these symptoms, many affected individuals have social difficulties and experience feelings of isolation.[13] While the condition is not entirely preventable, studies have shown that if a woman takes 400 µg of folic acid daily throughout her pregnancy, the chances of her child developing spina bifida are reduced by 70%.[14] Given that the expense and inconvenience of taking a tablet are extremely minimal, this would qualify as a small sacrifice made by the mother for the purposes of giving her child a much better chance at avoiding a bad life as a result of developing spina bifida.

An example of a slightly more moderate sacrifice would be a woman already infected with rubella or who has not been vaccinated against the disease. Contracting rubella during pregnancy or becoming pregnant while infected causes severe disabilities in the child including cataracts, deafness, and heart, lung, and brain abnormalities. If a woman has rubella she will have to wait until the infection passes before becoming pregnant. Or, if she has not been immunized against it, she will have to have the

---

[13] Spina Bifida Association, http://www.spinabifidaassociation.org/ (accessed February 21, 2023).

[14] Spina Bifida Association, "Folic Acid," https://www.spinabifidaassociation.org/resource/folic-acid/#-pbcJump (accessed February 21, 2023).

vaccination in order to ensure that she does not endanger her child. Whilst these are still small sacrifices relative to the negative effects on the child, they are still more significant than in the spina bifida case. A woman is potentially inconvenienced by having to delay conception, and having an injection is a more invasive and painful medical procedure than simply swallowing a tablet. Nonetheless, it is still at most only a moderate sacrifice.

Thus far we have been speaking of relatively minor sacrifices on the part of the rescuer/parent—taking pills or waiting a short time to have a child. However, one might think that in the case of procreation the sacrifices that can be required to avoid creating a person with a very bad life are much greater than 'minimal' or even moderate. Where the rescue and procreation cases differ is that *ex hypothesi* in the rescue case we have no special relationship or obligation to the person being rescued. Indeed, we may not even know who they are (for example, when donating money to help the developing world's poor). When we are rescuing a person, not only might it be the case that we do not have any special relationship or obligation to that person, but we are also presumably not directly causally responsible for their predicament. As a result, we cannot be asked to make very serious sacrifices in order to rescue them since this might put our own well-being in danger.

However, when creating new people, the parents *do* stand in a special relationship with respect to the child. Robert Goodin argues that it is the vulnerability and helplessness of the child that beget special parental responsibilities.[15] By responsibilities Goodin is referring to the requirement to provide the necessities of life to the child until the child is able to provide for themselves. Although he is referring to parents' responsibilities to already born children, the argument can also be extended to the act of creation. Whatever child you create is completely vulnerable to the conditions in which

---

[15] Robert E. Goodin (1985), "Vulnerabilities and Responsibilities: An Ethical Defense of the Welfare State," *American Political Science Review* 79(3).

they are created, so parents have special obligations when choosing how and when to procreate. Moreover, there are many people who believe that it is not just the vulnerability of the child that grounds special duties. The deliberate choice to have a child creates a special obligation since the parent was directly responsible for that child's creation and (a significant part of) the quality of life that the child will have.[16] It is plausible, therefore, that since the parent is freely choosing to bring a child into existence, they can be required to make more than 'moderate' sacrifices to ensure that the resulting child does not have a very bad life. I want to resist this conclusion, but some readers may think my reason is merely semantic. I will argue that sometimes the sacrifice required to avoid creating someone with a less than sufficiently good life may be to abstain from procreation at all, but that this is (usually, but not always) only a moderate sacrifice. My concern with requiring 'severe' sacrifices is that what those sacrifices might be could be unacceptable—for example, forced sterilization or other painful or invasive medical procedures.

Imagine a couple knows that they carry both carry a gene that will pass along to their child a disorder that caused him to have very bad life. Assume further that the only way to prevent a child from being born with a very bad life is for the couple to abstain from reproducing at all. To some, this may seem like more than just a moderate sacrifice.

It is true that having children is an entrenched part of what gives many people's lives meaning and value. Parents have personal reasons to want to have their own biological children—a desire for physical, familial, or psychological resemblance; expression of love of one's partner; immortality; the desire to experience pregnancy or witness the birth of one's child.[17] Ultimately, though, it

---

[16] For historical examples of a similar argument, see Henry Sidgwick (1874), *The Methods of Ethics*, 7th ed. (Macmillan); J. S. Mill (1863), "Utilitarianism," in *Mill: Utilitarianism and Other Essays*, ed. M. Warnock (Collins).

[17] Tina Rulli (2016), "Preferring a Genetically-Related Child," *Journal of Moral Philosophy* 13. Rulli also outlines several impersonal reasons for preferring genetically

is the *rearing* of children that is the primary good of parenthood. Parents have two reasons: a reason to want to create and parent a genetically related child and a reason to want to parent a child. Tina Rulli discusses the reasons for preferring a genetically related child in the course of arguing that only one—the desire to experience pregnancy—can ground a permission to procreate rather than adopt where infant adoption is available, and even then only once, because the desire to experience pregnancy is fulfilled after one child. This is because, for Rulli, the extreme needs of parentless children outweigh these reasons for desiring a genetically related child, which are "too trivial, presuppose the value of the genetic connection, are inappropriate in a normative parental context, or fail to make a relevant distinction between genetic and adopted children."[18] If these reasons cannot justify our failing to benefit an existing child in need, why should they justify *creating* a child who will have an insufficiently good life?

It seems implausible to accord priority to a person's wish to have biological children over a child having a decent life. Therefore, in cases where the only way to reproduce biologically is to create a child with a bad life, the parent's reason to reproduce is outweighed by the child's reason not to endure pain, suffering, etc. This is because the other, general good of parenthood is still available to the parents through adoption, making the sacrifice only the biological component, a sacrifice which is merely moderate and not severe. A child could therefore reasonably reject a principle that allowed his parents to create him knowing that he would have a bad life.

Some readers may bristle at this last statement. It may seem odd to say that a child could reasonably reject a principle that caused him to exist, albeit with a bad life, since if it were not for the principle, he would not have existed at all. To understand why this is so,

---

related children, such as the intrinsic value of a genetic connection and the value of *creating* a child.

[18] Ibid., 697.

it is important to revisit several points made earlier in the book. As I argued in Chapter 2, a person can have a *pro tanto* reason to reject a principle even if it caused them to exist if there were other reasons to reject the principle—in this case the pain caused by the genetic disorder or disease. Considering this situation from the perspective of the parent and their reasons may also help. We judge that a person has acted wrongly if they act upon an unacceptable reason or fail to recognize countervailing reasons. The parents' reason for reproducing in this situation is the desire to have a biological child, but if they choose to do so, they would be failing to recognize the countervailing reason that a person has for wanting to avoid a painful life and giving their own desires excessive weight. 'Never existing' is not a countervailing reason that needs to be considered by the parents.

The *Bad Lives* principle appears to prevent most instances of the creation of less than sufficiently good lives. However, I have deliberately left it open to the possibility that there *could* be a sacrifice deemed severe enough to outweigh the suffering of the person who will live a bad life. For example, if the only way to prevent a child from being born with a very bad life were to painfully sterilize a woman against her will and preclude her from adopting a child, this *may* be considered severe enough to render the creation of the child permissible—I am not sure. However, what is key is that procreation would be permissible only if the painful involuntary sterilization were the *only* way to prevent the bad life from being created. If there were other, non-objectionable ways to prevent it, there would still be an obligation to pursue these other means.

Good Lives

We have already seen that there is no duty to create the best *possible* child, but is it enough if we merely ensure that the children we create have sufficiently good lives? That is, is there a duty to do better than that, even though there is not a duty to create the best possible child?

Once resulting children are sure to have at least adequately good lives, I believe that the procreative obligations of parents are less straightforwardly defined. The question to answer now is whether it is supererogatory or obligatory to create a child with an even better quality of life when regardless of what you do you will have a child with at least a decent quality of life.

In the same way that *Rescue* was used to consider our obligations to children with bad lives, a principle analogous to *Helpfulness* will guide us in discovering our obligations (if any) when any child we could have is sure to have at least a decent life—or, in sufficientarian terms, at or above the sufficiency threshold. At this point parents are not required to make as large sacrifices in order to create even better-off children. This does not mean that a parent is never morally required to try to create the better quality of life, because the reasons to require them to do are still balanced against the other interests they may have.

Consider a woman who is deciding whether to have a child now or wait a month and have a child with a higher quality of life. No matter what choice the woman makes, the child's quality of life will be at least sufficiently good. Would it be wrong for a woman to choose to have a merely decently well-off child rather than wait one month (or incur another type of minor sacrifice)[19] and be able to create a better-off child?

The most helpful way to answer the question is to look at the reasons a parent has for both options. If the parent's reason not to wait is quite insignificant, like wanting the child to have a particular birthday or mere impatience, this may not be enough to justify not waiting, since the interest a child has in having a higher than decent

---

[19] Waiting to conceive is, of course, not the only type of sacrifice a parent might make. Other examples could include incurring extra health burdens, monetary costs, or inconvenience, or having to invest more time and energy into the procreative process.

quality of life must be taken into account and the parent would be sacrificing nothing of significance by waiting. On the other hand, if she has a somewhat weighty reason for wanting to have a child right away rather than waiting, it may be sufficient to justify having the child with the lower quality of life. For example, perhaps she knows that waiting will cause some permanent physical damage to her body. If she has the decently well-off child now, she will not sustain this damage and will be healthy, but if she does wait to have the child with the higher quality of life, she will have to deal with moderate pain for the rest of her life. This reason may be sufficient to justify having the child with the lower quality of life since she cannot be asked to make so great a sacrifice to create someone even better off when the child who would be created without the sacrifice is already sure to have at least a sufficiently good quality of life.[20] This balance changes according to the sacrifice being asked of the parent and the benefit that stands to be gained by the child.

Since the nature and strength of the sacrifices required to benefit an above-threshold child will differ depending on individual circumstances, it is impossible to specify a precise principle that would cover parents' obligations in all situations. However, I claim that the following general principle would be non-rejectable:

> *Good Lives*: Parents must create the best possible child—if the worst possible child will have a decent life—if the sacrifice required to do so would be less significant than the anticipated extra quality of life gained.

This means that when the creation of a child with a better life would be possible but would require more sacrifice of the parent than benefit to the child, it would be supererogatory to do so. It is impossible to specify every level or type of sacrifice that parents may be

---

[20] Of course, many women will choose to take on significant sacrifices, even death, for the sake of their future children.

required to make for children who will, regardless, live relatively normal lives. Scanlon himself thinks that judgements of this sort must always be made and that no plausible theory could avoid the need for such judgements. My claim is that the strength of reasons changes as the expected quality of life of the prospective child changes.

The reasons a child has to want to not be created with a very bad life are extremely strong and grounded in the fact that any such child would not have a sufficiently good life. Because of this, any reasons the parent could have for creating such a child would have to be extremely strong in order to justify creating a child at that level, and they would be required to take on severe sacrifices in order to prevent doing so. In the same way, but at the other end of the quality-of-life spectrum, when a child would live a sufficiently good life, any benefits that could be given to him/her must also be weighed against the sacrifices a parent would have to make in order to accrue these benefits. If the sacrifices are minor relative to the anticipated extra well-being for a child, then it would not be possible to justify not doing so, but if the sacrifices are disproportionately high, then it would be supererogatory.

The aim of this chapter has been to produce general principles governing procreative choices. The application of these principles in certain real-world scenarios has some interesting implications about everyday reproductive decisions. These will be discussed in Chapter 7.

5
Optimal Population Size

'Population size' can mean two things. First, it could mean the total number of people, including past people, who have lived and will ever live. Some might think it would be a good thing for this number to be as big as possible since that would mean as many people as possible got the chance to experience life/existence. I disagree with that view, but this is neither here nor there because it is not the meaning I have in mind in this chapter. Rather, I mean the second conception, which is the number of people who exist at any particular time. In the *intra*generational context the population size is given. To state the obvious, the world's population at any given moment is whatever it is. It is a distinctive feature of the *inter*generational context, however, that the number of people who will exist at some future time is *not* fixed. Many of our choices directly affect how many people will be born (for example, when a couple chooses to have four children instead of one), but other decisions can affect population size indirectly (like a government's pro- or anti-natalist policies, which incentivize or discourage procreation, respectively). Other human choices can also unexpectedly affect population size. Anthropogenic climate change is expected to significantly affect people's ways of life and life choices, which will undoubtedly affect future population size.[1]

---

[1] Non-anthropogenic events can of course also affect the number of people who exist/will exist by killing many people (e.g., a massive earthquake) or by making parts of the Earth hostile to further human life. However, assuming these events are random and not the result of human activities/choices, I won't consider them here since my focus is on the population size we ought to choose, not the one that is chosen for us through random natural occurrences.

The smallest possible population size is zero and the largest is the greatest number of people that can survive on the Earth at any one time, no matter how poor their quality of life may be. Life in the largest possible population size would be unthinkable. There would be never-ending competition for scarce resources, constant hunger, and likely war. If we assume that living like this would constitute lives not worth living, we can eliminate it as a viable 'optimal' population size. Even the most dedicated total utilitarian would reject it since the total utility would be negative: lots of people would get the 'opportunity' to exist, but their lives would be full of suffering. Although we can reject this population size, there is one somewhat close to it that cannot be dismissed so quickly, which is a population so large that people live lives that are worth living, but barely—i.e., Parfit's repugnant conclusion. These two extremes—human extinction and the repugnant conclusion—are considered by many philosophers and non-philosophers alike to be counterintuitive, and consequently, theories that endorse, or at least imply, these conclusions are thought to be weakened. Many philosophers are also interested in determining what the *optimal* population size is, between these two possibilities.[2]

My claim will be that a contractualist should reject almost all cases of human extinction and the repugnant conclusion, and permit many population sizes that fall between those ends. My ultimate conclusion is that there is no 'optimal' population size, but a spectrum of permissiveness, where principles advocating a given population size could not be reasonably rejected. Deciding between various populations within this realm should be made on the basis

---

[2] Hilary Greaves (2022), "Optimum Population Size," in *The Oxford Handbook of Population Ethics*, ed. Gustaf Arrhenius, Krister Bykvist, Tim Campbell, and Elizabeth Finneron-Burns (Oxford University Press); Aisha Dasgupta and Sir Partha Dasgupta (2022), "Population Overshoot," in *The Oxford Handbook of Population Ethics*, ed. Gustaf Arrhenius, Krister Bykvist, Tim Campbell, and Elizabeth Finneron-Burns (Oxford University Press).

of the strength of reasons—the burdens that would be incurred as a result of that size and the benefits that would be accrued.

Human Extinction

There seems to be a fairly widespread thought that it would be bad or wrong for humans to become extinct, as evidenced by the amount of research undertaken to avoid such an outcome by research institutes such as the Future of Humanity Institute at Oxford, the Centre for the Study of Existential Risk at Cambridge, and a relatively new focus on 'longtermism' within the (mostly) Effective Altruism community.[3] In actual fact I think the question of what 'human extinction' is or means can be quite complicated,[4] but for my purposes here I am going to consider it in its simplest and most obvious terms—when there are no longer any members of the species *Homo sapiens* living on Earth. Let's call the principle in question *Human Extinction*:

> *Human Extinction:* It is permissible to allow or cause human extinction to occur.

There are various reasons one might object to this principle.

Reasons to Object to Human Extinction
Preventing Life
One reason to object to human extinction lies in the value of human life itself. The thought here might be that it is a good thing for people to exist and enjoy happy lives, and extinction would

---

[3] William MacAskill (2022), *What We Owe the Future* (Basic Books); Toby Ord (2020), *The Precipice: Existential Risk and the Future of Humanity* (Bloomsbury).
[4] Elizabeth Finneron-Burns (forthcoming), "Humanity: Its Constitution, Value and Extinction," *The Monist*.

deprive (future) people of enjoying this good. The 'good' in this case could be understood in at least two ways. According to the first, one might believe that you benefit a person by bringing them into existence, or at least that it is good *for that person* that they come to exist. The second is that good lives add positive value or utility to the world. More lives mean more good, and extinction means no more of that good.

An example of this view can be found in a passage from the *Effective Altruism* blog post by Peter Singer, Nick Beckstead, and Matt Wage:

> If we fail to prevent our extinction, we will have blown the opportunity to create something truly wonderful: an astronomically large number of generations of human beings living rich and fulfilling lives, and reaching heights of knowledge and civilization that are beyond the limits of our imagination.[5]

The authors are claiming that there is intrinsic value in creating future people and that it would be a very bad thing if we did not do so. The best-known author of the post, Peter Singer, is a prominent utilitarian, so it is not surprising that he would lament the potential lack of future human lives per se. However, it is not just utilitarians who share this view, even if only implicitly. Stephen Gardiner (in published work)[6] and Martin O'Neill (in conversation), for example, both sympathetic to contract theory, also find it intuitive that we should want more generations to have the opportunity to exist, assuming that they have lives worth living, and I think it's likely that many other people, philosophers or otherwise, share their intuition.

---

[5] Nick Beckstead, Peter Singer, and Matt Wage (2013), "Preventing Human Extinction," *Effective Altruism* (blog), https://forum.effectivealtruism.org/posts/tXoE6wrEQv7GoDivb/preventing-human-extinction.

[6] Stephen Gardiner (2009), "A Contract on Future Generations," in *Intergenerational Justice*, ed. Axel Gosseries and Lukas Meyer (Oxford: Oxford University Press).

When we talk about future lives being 'prevented', we are saying that a possible person or a set of possible people who could potentially have existed will now never actually come to exist. To say that it is wrong to prevent people from existing could either mean that a possible person could reasonably reject a principle that permitted us not to create them, or that the forgone value of their life provides a reason for rejecting any principle that permits extinction.

To make the first claim we would have to argue that a possible person could reasonably reject any principle that prevented their existence, on the grounds that it prevented *them* in particular from existing. However, I have already argued that this is not plausible and it cannot be wrong to fail to bring particular people into existence. No one acts wrongly when they fail to create another person, and writ large, it would not be wrong if everybody decided to exercise their prerogative not to create new people and, potentially, cause human extinction.

One might respond here by saying that although it may be permissible for one person to fail to create a new person, it is not permissible if *everyone* does so because human lives have value and allowing human extinction would be to forgo a huge amount of value in the world. This takes us to the second way we might reject a principle allowing extinction, which is that the forgone value of human life provides us with a reason for rejecting any principle that prevents it.

Many philosophers acknowledge that the only, or at least the best, way to think about the value of possible people's lives is impersonally.[7] Jeff McMahan, for example, writes that "at the time of one's choice there is no one who exists or will exist independently of that choice for whose sake one could be acting in causing him

---

[7] Derek Parfit (1984), *Reasons and Persons* (Clarendon Press); Reiman (2007), "Being Fair to Future People: The Non-Identity Problem in the Original Position," *Philosophy & Public Affairs* 35(1); Jeff McMahan (2009), "Asymmetries in the Morality of Causing People to Exist," in *Harming Future Persons: Ethics, Genetics and the Non-Identity Problem*, ed. Melinda A. Roberts and David Wasserman (Springer).

or her to exist . . . it seems therefore that any reason to cause or not to cause an individual to exist . . . is best considered an impersonal rather than individual-affecting reason."[8] Along similar lines, one might appeal to the value that is lost or at least forgone when we fail to bring into existence the next generation (or several next generations) of people with lives worth living. Since, *ex hypothesi*, lives worth living have positive value, it is better to create more such lives, and worse to create fewer. Human extinction by definition is the creation of no future lives.

Both of these appeals depend on the impersonal value of human life, but impersonal values are not on their own grounds for rejecting principles. Scanlon himself says that although we have a strong reason not to destroy existing human lives, this reason doesn't "flow from the thought that it is a good thing for there to be more human life rather than less" (104). As we know by now, a principle can't be reasonably rejected unless there is some impact on a *person*. So neither the impersonal value of creating a particular person nor the impersonal value of human life writ large could on its own provide a reason for rejecting *Human Extinction*.

Loss of Intelligent Life, Civilization, and Progress

Another reason we might want to reject the principle is based on the loss that would occur from losing the only (known) form of rational life and the knowledge and civilization that that form of life has created. One thought here could be that just as some might consider it wrong to destroy an individual human heritage monument like the Sphinx, it would also be wrong if the advances made by humans over the past few millennia were lost or prevented from progressing. A related argument is made by those who feel that there is something special about humans' capacity for rationality which is valuable in itself. Since humans are the only intelligent life

---

[8] McMahan, "Asymmetries in the Morality of Causing People to Exist": 52.

that we know of, it would be a loss, in itself, to the world for that to end.

I admit that I struggle to fully appreciate this thought. It seems to me that Henry Sidgwick was correct in thinking that these things are only important insofar as they are important to humans. If there is no form of intelligent life in the future, who would there be to lament its loss since only intelligent life is able to appreciate intelligence? Similarly, if there is no one with the rational capacity to appreciate historic monuments and civil progress, who would there be to be negatively affected by or even notice the loss?

Even if there is nothing special about human rationality, just as some people try to prevent the extinction of nonhuman animal species, we might think that we ought also to prevent human extinction for the sake of biodiversity. The thought is that it would be somehow bad for the world if there were no more humans, even though there would be no one for whom it is bad.

All of these reasons—loss of civilization, intelligent life, the intrinsic value of species—are impersonal so there is no standpoint from which these reasons could be used to reasonably reject *Human Extinction*.

Pain and Death

Most of the ways human extinction could come about result in physical pain and/or premature death for the people who exist at the time the extinction occurs. It's not hard to imagine examples in which extinction causes premature death. A nuclear war or winter that killed everyone is a clear—and, sadly, becoming less improbable—example of such a case. Obviously some instances of premature death cannot themselves be reasons to reject a principle. Everyone dies eventually, some earlier than the standard expected lifespan, such as from accidents or incurable cancers. A disease is not a moral agent, so it doesn't make sense, in the strict sense, to say that it was wrong that a person died of cancer.[9]

---

[9] Absent human factors like malpractice or reasons a patient was unable to access available life-saving care.

However, the fact that a principle would reduce a person's well-being gives that person a reason to reject it. Some philosophers argue that death is a harm to the person who dies, whilst others argue that it's not, so it isn't yet settled whether premature death is a setback to well-being. Regardless of who is correct in this debate, being caused to die prematurely can be a reason to reject a principle when it fails to show respect to the person as a rational agent.

Recognising others as rational beings with interests involves seeing a reason to preserve life and prevent death (104). This respect for life is a respect for the people living, not a respect for human life in the abstract. This means that we can sometimes fail to protect human life without acting wrongfully if we still respect the person living. Imagine a person who faces a life of unending and extreme pain so bad that she wishes to end it through suicide. The suicidal person does not show a lack of respect for her own life by seeking to end it because the person whose life it is has no reason to want it to go on. This is important because it emphasizes the fact that the respect for human life is person-affecting. It's wrong to murder not because of the impersonal disvalue of death in general, but because taking someone's life without their permission shows disrespect to that person. This is why it doesn't really matter who is right in the 'Is death a harm?' debate. Even if death turns out not to harm the person who died, ending their life without their consent shows disrespect to them, and a person has reason to reject a principle that allowed their premature death. This is as true in the case of death in the course of human extinction as it is for death from murder.

Human extinction could also cause physical pain to existing people, even if it doesn't kill them. Imagine, for example, surgically removing everybody's reproductive organs in order to prevent procreation. Or a nuclear bomb that miraculously didn't kill anyone, but did painfully render them infertile through illness or injury. These are cases in which physical pain was inflicted on people and the extinction came about as a result of this painful incident, not through death.

It seems uncontroversial that the infliction of physical pain could be a reason to reject a principle allowing human extinction. Although well-being is not the only reason to reject principles, it plays a significant role, and indeed, most principles are likely to be rejectable due to negative impacts on well-being, physical or otherwise (more on the latter in the next section).

One might wonder at this point whether it is actually the involuntariness of the pain that is grounds for reasonable rejection, rather than the physical pain itself, because not all pain that people suffer is involuntary. Many acts cause can physical pain but are not rejectable—base jumping and surgery, for example. On the other hand, pushing someone off a cliff or cutting him with a scalpel against his will are clearly rejectable acts. The difference between the two cases is that in the former, the person having the pain inflicted has consented to that pain or risk of pain. My view is that they cannot be separated in these cases, and it is involuntary physical pain that is the grounds for reasonable rejection, not the pain itself. The fact that a principle would allow non-consensual physical harm gives a person who would be subjected to that harm a reason to reject the principle.

Of course, the mere fact that the principle causes involuntary physical harm or premature death is not necessarily sufficient to be sure that it is reasonably rejectable because there might be countervailing reasons. In the case of *Human Extinction*, what countervailing reasons might be offered? One could be that humans are such a harm to the natural environment that the world would be a better place if there were no humans in it. It could be the case that humans should be considered a hindrance to the world rather than a benefit to it, given that we have been largely responsible for the extinction of many other species, pollution, and, most recently, climate change, all of which have negatively affected the natural environment in ways we are only just beginning to understand. The fact that human extinction would improve the natural environment (or at least prevent it from degrading further) is a countervailing reason in favour of extinction that must be weighed against the reasons held by humans not to experience pain or premature death. However, the good of the environment as just described is, by definition, not a personal reason. Just like the loss of rational life and civilization, it cannot be a reason on its own to countervail the strong personal reasons people have to avoid pain or death.[10] The good of the environment, then, cannot countervail against personal reasons people at the time of extinction would have on the grounds of pain and premature death.

Psychological Pain
Although the fact that there will not be any future people is an impersonal reason, it could give rise to personal reasons to reject *Human Extinction*.

First, there would be a negative effect on those people who would have wanted to have children but cannot. While it is no means universal, it is fair to say that a good proportion of people feel a strong pull towards reproduction. Samuel Scheffler describes this pull as a "desire for a personalized relationship with the future."[11] Procreation is a widely held desire, and the joys of parenthood are ones that many people wish to experience. For these people, knowing that they will not have descendants could create a sense of despair and pointlessness of life. Furthermore, the inability to procreate because a principle or policy prevents you (for instance, through bans or physical interventions) would be a significant infringement of what we

[10] Göran Duus-Otterström suggested to me the following reply. He points out, correctly, that although impersonal reasons cannot on their own provide reasons for rejecting a principle, they may create other personal reasons. He cites Crake in Margaret Atwood's novel *Oryx & Crake*. Crake embarks on a genocidal mission to rid the Earth of human beings in order to benefit the environment. Duus-Otterström suggests that the impersonal reason to preserve the environment is so important to Crake's ability to live a fulfilling life that it creates a personal reason for Crake's programme. However, even if one wants to accept that Crake's reason is personal, it must still be weighed against the personal reasons of those who would be killed as a result of his programme. A person's reason not to be involuntarily killed must surely outweigh another person's reason to want to preserve the environment.
[11] Samuel Scheffler (2012), *Death and the Afterlife* (Oxford University Press): 31.

consider to be a basic right to control what happens to your body. Knowing that you will not have descendants could cause significant psychological harm, even if there is no associated physical harm.

Second, there may be a generalized sense of despair or hopelessness that there will be no more humans and that your projects will end with you. Even those who did not feel a strong desire to procreate themselves might feel that projects and goals for the future lose their meaning because many of these projects and goals are at least partly future-oriented. Why bother continuing the search for a cure for cancer if it can't be found before humans go extinct, or if there will be no future people to benefit from it when it's found? Politics, artistic pursuits, and philosophy may also lose their meaning and purpose when confronted by extinction. Even more extreme, through the words of the character Theo Faron, P. D. James says in her novel *The Children of Men* that "without the hope of posterity for our race if not for ourselves, without the assurance that we being dead yet live, all pleasures of the mind and senses sometimes seem to me no more than pathetic and crumbling defences shored up against our ruins."[12]

Even if James' claim is a bit extreme and *all* pleasures would not be lost, I agree with Scheffler in finding it plausible that the knowledge that extinction was coming and that there would be no more people would have at least a general depressive effect on people's motivation and confidence in the value of and joy in their activities.[13] Both sources of psychological harm are personal reasons for existing people to reject *Human Extinction*.

An Obligation to Procreate?

We've seen the grounds on which a principle permitting human extinction could be reasonably rejected. To complete the

---

[12] P. D. James (2006), *The Children of Men* (Random House).
[13] Scheffler, *Death and the Afterlife*: 43.

picture, though, we also need to look at its alternative—a principle prohibiting human extinction. On the straightforward understanding of what human extinction is, the way to prevent it is for people to procreate. In a scenario where extinction happened because no one wanted to have children, the only way to prevent extinction would be to require people to reproduce. Could a principle requiring people to have children be reasonably rejected?

Obligatory Creation: It is morally required to procreate in order to avoid human extinction.

There are a number of objections to this principle. Starting with current people, those who would be required to have children could reasonably reject the principle because it conflicts with other important interests and entitlements, particularly their reproductive autonomy. Even if a person would have wanted a child anyway and their life is improved by having one, a principle that *requires* a person to have a child, that is, that makes it *morally wrong* not to, removes the element of choice. No longer is a person morally free to pursue their personal aims and preferences with respect to reproduction. Even if the person did want to have a child and feels their life is improved by the existence of that child, they could reasonably reject the principle since it took the choice out of their hands. Of course, saying that something is morally required does not mean that there will be an *actual* interference with people's actual freedom to choose—after all, it is a moral principle, not a legal one, and people may choose not to comply with it. However, the fact that an act is wrong gives a person good reason not to perform it. In this case, knowing that failing to create a child would be wrong would give a person a good reason to create that child, and it would be impossible to exercise autonomy and act morally at the same time.[14]

---

[14] More precisely, but more cumbersomely, knowing that failing to create a child with a good life would be wrong gives the person good reason not to fail to create the child. Whew, that's a mouthful!

It could be objected that in Chapter 4 I argued that in most cases it was impermissible to knowingly create a child with a bad life. This too is an infringement of reproductive autonomy. It is true that in both cases there is an interference in autonomy, but the balance of reasons again comes into play. In the previous case autonomy was not a strong enough reason to outweigh a child's reason not to want to be created with a bad life. What is the reason militating against autonomy in this case? On a micro scale it would be the child who is created (and otherwise would not have been), and on a macro level, it is the continuation of 'humanity.' But we've already seen that the former is not a relevant reason in contractualist justification, and we have determined that the value of humanity itself (intelligent life, cultural progress, etc.) is an impersonal reason.

Balancing the claims in favour of and against *Obligatory Creation*, it becomes clear that it could be reasonably rejected by current people who do not wish to have children, whereas the alternative, in which we are not obliged to have children to prevent extinction, is not rejectable. Rejecting *Obligatory Creation* as it has been stated here does not mean that it is *never* obligatory to procreate, just that it is not required *in order to prevent human extinction*. Indeed, there might be cases in which it may be required to procreate. One example that comes to mind is that of a sick child. If a 'saviour sibling' could be created to provide a lifesaving bone marrow transplant, it is conceivable that the parents might be required to do so. I will briefly discuss saviour siblings in Chapter 7, but the key point for now is that in this example, the parents' autonomy is being weighed against another *personal* reason—saving the life of a sick child—and not something impersonal like the value of humanity or the fact that the future sibling would have a good life.[15]

---

[15] See Caleb Althorpe and Elizabeth Finneron-Burns (forthcoming), "Are Saviour Siblings a Special Case in Procreative Ethics?" *Journal of Ethics and Social Philosophy*.

Implications for the Permissibility of Human Extinction

I've examined four reasons to reject human extinction and argued that only two could be the basis for reasonably rejecting a principle like *Human Extinction* that permits it:

(1) Existing people would ensure physical pain and/or premature death.
(2) Existing people would endure psychological harms such as depression and the loss of meaning in their pursuits and projects.

The implication of my argument is that whether or not contractualism supports principles that lead to human extinction depends primarily on the way in which extinction would come about and, more specifically, its effects on the people who exist at the time. This means that human extinction is only wrong insofar as it negatively impacts existing people's interests.

Extinction from involuntary sterilizations and nuclear holocaust would be wrong because they were involuntary, were potentially painful, and led to premature death. So too would cases where we simply failed to prevent extinction, despite knowing that it would cause harm to the people who exist. An example of this could be an asteroid hurtling towards Earth. Once it hits, it will prematurely kill everyone on Earth. Luckily, we have discovered how to divert asteroids in advance so that they do not make contact with our planet in the future. It would be wrong for us not to divert the asteroid since whoever will exist at the time of its impact would have a strong reason to reject a principle that permitted us to fail to divert the asteroid.

But if a principle permitting human extinction had no involuntary negative impacts on existing people's interests, it would not be rejectable, and the resulting extinction would not be wrong. Even if extinction happened in a painful way, voluntarily incurred pain is not necessarily a reason for rejection since a person does not have to reject a principle even if it objectively lowers their well-being (213–18). If there were a way of causing human extinction that was universally (all those who exist when the extinction occurs) voluntary, and involved no other infringements of rights or autonomy, a principle permitting it would not be rejectable. It is possible to imagine physically painless methods of human extinction, but I struggle to imagine one that would be universally voluntary. Nonetheless, it is theoretically possible, and if it became reality, it would not be wrong.

One final form of extinction to be considered is one that is caused painlessly and without anyone knowing about it (thus avoiding physical and emotional harms). The person enacting such a policy would be showing disrespect to those who were impacted since the agreement in contractualism is only hypothetical. It is not necessary that the impacted parties *know* that they are being impacted. As Rahul Kumar explains, permitting others to make decisions about how another person's body may be used is grounds for reasonable rejection, regardless of whether or not harm or the risk of harm is being imposed, because "each individual has good reason to want this kind of decision-making discretion to be solely her own (regardless of whether or not her body would in fact be used by others were it (to even in part be) ceded)."[16] In any case, there would have to be very strong, personal reasons in favour of the sterilization for it to overcome the possible objections of the people being affected.

In most cases of potential human extinction, then, it looks as though contractualism is consistent with the intuition I laid out at the start—that there would be something wrong with causing or allowing human extinction. Interestingly, however, the wrongness is grounded not in the forgoing of potential future lives, but in the interests of the people who would exist at the time of the extinction.

---

[16] Rahul Kumar (2015), "Risking and Wronging," *Philosophy & Public Affairs* 43(1).

However, we cannot sweep under the rug the two cases in which extinction would *not* be wrong:

(1) When the cause of extinction is completely non-anthropogenic and/or unavoidable.
(2) When the extinction is universally (by all affected) voluntary.

Is it a problem that we cannot explain the wrongness of human extinction in these scenarios? I don't think it is. It's not clear in (1) how an unavoidable natural disaster could plausibly be described as 'wrong' when 'wrong' seems in almost every moral theory to mean something that was done through human choice when there was an option not to.

What of (2), though? It is possible that the extinction in (2) could be impersonally *bad* since it prevents new people from enjoying happy lives and destroys the only form of intelligent life (that we know of), but this is not the same as being wrong. Those unconvinced by the contractualist framework to begin with may want to throw the baby out with the bathwater and declare that this is evidence that contractualism simply can't supply an adequate response to the problem of human extinction since, in some scenarios, it finds it not to be wrong.

But those of us more sympathetic to the theory (and reader, I hope that by this point you are one of us) have two options. The first is to bite the bullet and accept that (2) is not wrong, despite an apparent intuition to the contrary. Our intuition sets are often inconsistent and all theories have bullets to bite; contractualism is not unique in this regard. Wrongness has to do with relations between persons and how we ought to treat each other. In cases such as (2), no one is being treated unfairly or harmed in any way, so perhaps it is simply the case that there is no wrongdoing here.

The other option might be to claim that actually there *are* people being disrespected or harmed: past people. It could be argued that allowing human extinction frustrates past people's interests by not continuing their projects (either the project of continuing the human species itself or projects that can only continue by virtue of people continuing to exist). Scanlon does allow that any current, future, *or past* person constitutes a standpoint towards which justification makes sense. If it is in fact possible to frustrate a past person's interests or harm them, this might be a personal reason to reject principles that allow human extinction, even if every currently existing person were in favour. Perhaps a current person made a promise to their grandmother to carry on the family name. The promise may have a posthumous claim to the promiser keeping this promise and having children. I am sceptical of this possible solution, primarily because even if past people's interests can constitute personal reasons in this way, it seems unlikely that they would outweigh current people's much weightier (in my view) interest in personal autonomy and making decisions about one's own body. However, there is some disagreement about this last claim, so the matter is far from settled. I am open to the possibility that past people might be wronged through human extinction, but I have not yet seen a convincing explanation of how this would work.[17] Nonetheless, given the burgeoning philosophical interest in the ethics of human extinction, I am hopeful that one may one day be found.

The Repugnant Conclusion(s)

I now turn to the opposite extreme: the repugnant conclusion. As a reminder, the repugnant conclusion is:

> *Repugnant Conclusion*: For any possible large population A, whose members all have a very high quality of life, there must be

---

[17] For example, see Patrick Kaczmarek and SJ Beard (2020), "Human Extinction and Our Obligations to the Past," *Utilitas* 32(2), but also my reply, Elizabeth Finneron Burns (2022), "Human Extinction and Moral Worthwhileness," *Utilitas* 34(1).

some much larger imaginable population Z whose existence, if other things are equal, would be better, even though its members have lives that are barely worth living.[18]

As it has been stated above, the repugnant conclusion is an axiological claim about the relative value of two different populations, one large and the other larger. Parfit concludes that if we accept a total consequentialist view, we must accept that the larger population Z is better than the smaller population A. However, it does not necessarily follow that the fact of one state being better than another means that we are obligated to bring the better state into being. Although many people probably find the idea that Z is better than A troubling in itself, Mulgan believes that the primary intuitive objection to the repugnant conclusion actually comes from a normative, not axiological, statement:

Repugnant Obligation Conclusion: If any agent faces a choice between two actions whose outcomes correspond to Parfit's A-world and Z-world, then she ought to choose Z over A.[19]

For total utilitarians both the repugnant conclusion and repugnant obligation conclusion would be true, whereas other ethical theories could accept the descriptive component of the repugnant conclusion while also rejecting the implication that the betterness of world Z implies an obligation to choose it over A. This could, for example, be defended on the grounds that Z is *pro tanto* better than A, but that some other value or reason is present that allows one to opt for A.

Contractualism is not primarily concerned with ranking the betterness of different outcomes; rather, it is interested in what

---

[18] Parfit, *Reasons and Persons*: 388.
[19] Tim Mulgan (2006), *Future People: A Moderate Consequentialist Account of Our Obligations to Future Generations* (Clarendon Press): 61.

principles are rejectable and non-rejectable, and therefore what actions are permitted or not permitted. To that end, I will be concerned not with disputing the betterness of population A or Z, but with the *permissibility* of choosing either. Could it ever be required or even permissible to bring about population Z? I will argue that a principle that required or permitted bringing about the Z-world could be reasonably rejected, but since contractualism is essentially comparative, it is not enough simply to reject Z; it is also necessary to show that the alternative principle (bringing about population A instead) could not be reasonably rejected.

Populations A and Z

Population A should be understood to be an arbitrarily selected 'midsized' population that should be taken to reflect any population size between zero and population Z where all members of the population have at least a sufficiently good quality of life.

In population Z, the population size is as large as possible whilst still maintaining a quality of life just above the point at which life would no longer be worth living, but well below the sufficiency threshold. There are some philosophers who believe the repugnant conclusion is not actually repugnant and that we ought to happily accept its implications because we misunderstand what a life barely worth living would be like and assume it to be much worse than what most people already enjoy now. On the contrary, says Torbjörn Tännsjö, our lives are already barely worth living.[20] If our lives are already barely worth living, and we perceive our lives to be good, then there would be no reason to reject the repugnant conclusion: we are already living in population Z.

---

[20] Torbjörn Tännsjö (2002), "Why We Ought to Accept the Repugnant Conclusion," *Utilitas* 14.

Unsurprisingly, I disagree with Tännsjö. Most people, at least in the developed world, live lives that are fairly healthy, are economically prosperous, and include aspects of life other than simply working to survive (such as sport, art, culture, and so on). It seems to me that our lives could be substantially worse while still remaining worth living.

To counter this point, Tännsjö gives examples of people with acquired disabilities who describe their lives not as worse than before, but simply as different. His point is that even with the acquisition of a serious disability, people's lives are not made worse, and he uses this to argue that there is not as much space as we may think between lives that are 'not worth living' and the lives we live now.[21] This may be true, and indeed disability rights activists would almost certainly agree. However, it could also mean that we imagine acquiring a disability to be much worse than it actually is, and that this is just not a good example of a life that is barely worth living.

There are many other aspects of life that we believe make life better, such as sports, financial security, the arts, personal relationships, and so on. Surely a life devoid of all of these things would be worse than one with them—otherwise, why value them at all? Tännsjö might reply that this is an example of a life not worth living. Indeed, he believes that a large number of people in the developing world live lives that are not worth living, and argues that merely failing to commit suicide does not mean that a person deems their own life worth living for various reasons. I suggest, on the contrary, that if you asked a person in such a state, they would likely say that they do believe their life is worth living, in the same way that the newly disabled person does; that is, they have adapted to their circumstances, and believe their life to have value.[22] The fact that they see value in their life, however, does not negate the

---

[21] Ibid.
[22] In fact, saying that people in these countries 'see their lives have value' rather understates the case. The Cantril Ladder asks people to "imagine a ladder, with steps

fact that objectively their life is worse than the lives that other people enjoy.

In population Z resources would be scarce, government services would be overextended, and people would live in cramped conditions without food security. These conditions would be a significant burden for the people in population Z. Could a principle that brings about such a state be reasonably rejected?

Obligatory Repugnance

Dealing first with the question of whether it could ever be required to bring about population Z, I think the answer is quite clearly no. Given that I assume that we are not already living in population Z, to bring it about we would presumably need to reproduce at a higher rate than we are now. We would all need to create as many children as possible as long as they will have lives that are at least barely worth living. However, we have already seen there is no moral obligation to have a child, even if he or she would have a life worth living. Any policy that achieved population growth through a moral requirement to procreate would be reasonably rejectable by those who do not wish to have (more) children, and the possible people who are 'left out' of existence are not owed mutual justification.

---

numbered from 0 at the bottom to 10 at the top. The top of the ladder represents the best possible life for you and the bottom of the ladder represents the worst possible life for you. On which step of the ladder would you say you personally feel you stand at this time?" According to this measure, even in the Democratic Republic of Congo, which has suffered decades of war and hunger, the average self-reported life satisfaction score is 4.31/10. Although it is depressing that the average is so low, it is clear that people, even in the DRC, consider their lives to be worth living. For reference, in the United States, the richest country per capita in the world, the average score is only 6.98/10. Esteban Ortiz-Ospina and Max Roser (2017), "Happiness and Life Satisfaction," Our World in Data, https://ourworldindata.org/happiness-and-life-satisfaction.

Permissible Repugnance

Although bringing about population Z is not *required*, perhaps it is *permissible*. As I have argued throughout this book, a future person could reasonably reject a principle that left them with an insufficiently good life even if that principle also caused them in particular to exist. In the same way, the members of population Z could reasonably reject the policy that permitted extreme population growth on the grounds that it caused them to live in a condition of poverty and overcrowding or without the other positive components of life.

We also need to consider the perspective of the person trying to justify a particular principle. What reasons could current people give in support of a principle permitting population Z? There do not seem to be any admissible reasons. One reason in support of the principle is that population Z includes a lot of value in the form of extra lives that are worth living. This reason is inadmissible both because it is impersonal and also because it unacceptably aggregates the value of human lives (229–40).

Another reason that might be given is that it creates particular future people who would not otherwise have existed. But as I've argued before, a person cannot justify a principle to a future person on the grounds that it would cause them in particular to exist since the information about who in particular will exist is neither available to them at the time of acting nor within their control (what would it mean to get to decide whom to create?). On the larger scale, current people could also not justify a principle to the members of population Z on the grounds that it would cause those particular people to exist. It cannot be their reason for action, or a reason for justification to others.

However, in order to fully make the case against the permissibility of bringing about population Z, we must also show that the objections to the alternative—limiting the size of the population—are not stronger. If the natural rate of population growth were expected to create population Z, then the only way to prevent population Z would be by limiting population growth. Are there non-rejectable ways of preventing population Z?

One way of ensuring that the population does not grow too large is to limit the number of children individuals are permitted to have. We can use the size of the current population, expected mortality rates, available resources, etc. to determine the ideal size of the next generation. Once the number of children who should be born is determined, we will need to figure out how to distribute the number of children among people/families fairly. For the sake of fairness, in the first instance, it might make sense to limit each person to an equal number of permitted children. If a person does not wish to have any children, they can give their rights to another person to have an extra child—a kind of cap-and-trade system for children, if you will.

The distribution will likely not prevent most people from having more children than they would otherwise have had and therefore will be no burden at all, even if couples are limited to just one child each. In the United Kingdom in 2019, almost half of families had only one child anyway. Moreover, the national average is 1.8 live birth per woman, and 18% of British women have no children at all.[23] For the minority of people who would have liked to have more than one child, a policy like this is still not a significant burden. They are still able to enjoy the pleasures of parenthood if they choose.[24]

But one might object that *any* limitation on the number of children a person is permitted to have is a significant burden, regardless of the number of children they already have. To test this, consider

---

[23] Fertility statistics are generally tracked according to the number of children per woman, rather than per person or per family. Office of National Statistics (2020), "Childbearing for Women in England and Wales: 2019," https://www.ons.gov.uk/peopl epopulationandcommunity/birthsdeathsandmarriages/conceptionandfertilityrates/ bulletins/childbearingforwomenbornindifferentyearsenglandandwales/2019.

[24] It could be objected that being limited to one child would have a significant effect on a person's life if it prevented them being able to secure their future well-being in their old age, such as in cultures where it is the norm that children care for their ageing parents or work to contribute to the household's expenses (China's one-child policy springs to mind). My (perhaps unsatisfactory) response is that I am considering the question from

the following case. Ann and Andrew already have a child, whereas Barbara and Bob are childless. If both couples required a drug to become pregnant in the future, and there were only one dose of the drug, to which couple should it be given? I think most people would think that it should go to Barbara and Bob since without it they will have no children, whereas Ann and Andrew have already benefited from having a child. It is a much greater burden to deny someone the opportunity to have a first child than it is to deny a person the opportunity to have subsequent children. This is not to say that there is no burden incurred at all, simply that the burden is relatively minor.

There may be some circumstances in which it may not be permissible to limit population size, even if the resulting children will have insufficiently good lives. If the only way to prevent population Z from occurring were to ban some families from having even one child (if they wanted to), then the burdens incurred by those families would be significant and possibly enough to justify procreation. I say possibly because there may be alternative ways for people to enjoy the benefits of parenting without procreating themselves. In this example adoption is unlikely to be an option (since we have limited the number of children people can have, there is unlikely to be a significant number of adoptable children). But something like Anca Gheaus' proposal for 'child sharing,' where multiple people parent a child together, might be a solution.[25] Furthermore, some of the ways a population could be either reduced or limited that would be objectionable—like genocide, forced sterilizations, forced abortion, and so on—would constitute serious harms to the people affected, due either to the pain involved or the loss of autonomy.[26]

---

a Western perspective where this is not a cultural norm or necessity. If the same principle were put forward in a developing nation, the context there might well make it rejectable.

[25] Anca Gheaus (2019), "More Co-Parents, Fewer Children: Multiparenting and Sustainable Population," *Essays in Philosophy* 20(1).
[26] Not everyone thinks reproductive autonomy infringements are problematic. See Sarah Conly (2015), *One Child: Do We Have a Right to More?* (Oxford University Press).

If the population were limited according to these means, it would certainly be impermissible. However, what is important is that theoretically, limiting the number of children each family is morally permitted to have is, in most cases, permissible.

It seems, then, that a principle requiring or permitting population Z could be reasonably rejected by current people (who would have an unreasonable moral requirement to procreate) and/or by future people (who would be created with bad lives), and its alternative (limiting population size) could not.[27]

To briefly summarize the discussion about the repugnant conclusion so far, I have argued that a principle requiring or permitting the creation of population Z could be reasonably rejected. This means that if we think about the question of population size from a contractualist perspective, we see that the theory is not committed to either the repugnant conclusion or the repugnant obligation conclusion.

The final question is what this conclusion adds to contractualism's value as a theory of intergenerational ethics. As we've already seen, there are those who don't find the repugnant conclusion repugnant at all,[28] and those who don't think it is a 'knockdown' argument against a theory that implies it.[29] But those who do should see it as an asset of contractualism that the theory not only does not imply such a conclusion, but also explains why the conclusion is something we want to avoid, by expressing the question in terms of respect owed to others. What is wrong with the repugnant conclusion is the disrespect we show towards those who will live in population Z. To argue that it is better that many people live bad lives than for fewer people to live good lives is to show a disregard for the people who will end up suffering in population Z, preferring instead to

---

[27] Remember that those potential people who would have been born if population Z had been chosen do not have any objections to principles limiting population size.
[28] Tännsjö, "Why We Ought to Accept the Repugnant Conclusion."
[29] Stéphane Zuber et al. (2021), "What Should We Agree on About the Repugnant Conclusion?," *Utilitas* 33.

'bestow' existence on as many 'people' as possible, most of whom otherwise never would have existed and should not have been owed consideration in the first place.

So, What *Is* the Optimal Population Size?

What is the optimal population size? There isn't one. In most cases contractualism would permit neither the largest possible population nor the smallest population (i.e., extinction). Any population between these extremes (let's call it population X) that is proposed must be considered in light of the potential reasons to reject or accept it. The means by which that population size is brought about and the resulting quality of life for the people in it are particularly important. If the means of achieving population X and the resulting quality of life for the members of population X are not rejectable, then population X is permitted. Likewise, if they are rejectable, then population X (or at least the principle/policy leading to it) is impermissible and we have an obligation not to bring it about in the way proposed.

As in previous chapters, the sufficiency threshold also plays a role. The reasons current people have for bringing about population X must be balanced against the (very strong) reason the people in population X have for wanting to live sufficiently good lives. Therefore, unless there are very strong reasons for current people to create a population X that did not live sufficiently good lives, contractualism will always advocate a population size small/large enough that all members of the population have the opportunity to be above the sufficiency threshold.[30]

---

[30] I bear in mind that it is never possible to ensure that *every* member of a given population is above the sufficiency threshold due to factors outside of human control such as extremely painful medical conditions. What is important is that it is not the decision about population size itself that has caused people to live insufficiently good lives.

It may seem that effectively the spectrum of permissive population sizes is not actually between zero and population Z, but, rather, between zero and the largest population in which everyone is still sufficiently well off (let's call it population S). I want to resist this conclusion because one of the key virtues of contractualism is that it is context-sensitive. As I showed in Chapters 4 and 5, although sufficiency is a very weighty reason, it can, in some circumstances, be outweighed by other considerations. In the same way, it is possible that if the reasons of current people were weighty enough, they could be permitted to create a population in which people did not live sufficiently good lives (though those lives were still worth living).

Thus, contractualism allows us to choose population sizes between zero and enormous on the basis of the same considerations that have been present throughout the book. That is, we balance the sacrifices required to bring about the desired population with the benefits that stand to be gained by the people who will live in that population, and in particular, their opportunity to enjoy sufficiently good lives. So many factors affect the quality of our lives, and population size is just one of them. The optimal population is therefore constantly changing as our circumstances change, and contractualism gives us the flexibility to change with it.

6
Our Future Is Uncertain

Thus far I have described the principles I believe contractualism would endorse with respect to intergenerational resource distribution, procreative ethics, and population size. In these chapters I have either explicitly assumed that we knew certain facts about the future—how many future people there will be, how well off a particular child will end up, what resources future people will need for a sufficiently good life—or left the issue aside. But in the real world, we do not always know these things and there are many ways in which lack of knowledge can affect our moral obligations. So, it is time to address it.

Risk

Realistically, we often have only partial knowledge of what the consequences of our actions will be for future people, so we are faced with a choice between different probabilities. In this section I will consider what role the risk that a harm will occur plays in justifying our actions to future people.

Contractualism and Risk Imposition

Scanlon considers the permissibility of imposing risk on others briefly in the course of his larger discussion of generality and fairness (ch. 5, sec. 5). As we well know by now, when determining whether or not a principle could be reasonably rejected, we must consider the weightiness of the burdens it imposes on certain people and the importance of the benefits it offers to others. But if we do not also consider the *likelihood* of the respective burdens or benefits occurring, this could cause problems. Imagine, for instance that we are deciding between two principles. The first permits an action that has an exceptionally low likelihood of a very serious burden being imposed on someone, whereas the alternative principle permits an action with a very high likelihood of imposing a small burden. If we simply compare the relative potential burdens of the two principles with no regard to the probability of the burdens actually occurring, it would seem that the first principle could certainly be rejected despite the fact that its burden was extremely unlikely to occur, whereas there would be less reason to reject the second principle, which virtually guaranteed a burden, since that burden is of a smaller magnitude.

The first kind of case (low risk, high burden) occurs frequently in our daily lives. One popular example is the danger incurred by air travel.[1] Whenever an airplane flies above a populated area, there is a very slight risk that it will crash and kill people on the ground below. The potential burden to these people (death) is very serious but also extremely unlikely. On the other hand, the benefit incurred by those travelling on planes is moderate but virtually guaranteed to be enjoyed. Another common example of risky behaviour is driving a car. There is always a chance that a driver will cause a fatal accident to a pedestrian. The benefit to each driver of being permitted to use their vehicles is pretty high, but not as high as the potential burden suffered by an unlucky pedestrian. With no regard given to the likelihoods of the burdens/benefits being incurred, a principle allowing air travel or driving could be reasonably rejected since the

---

[1] See James Lenman (2008), "Contractualism and Risk Imposition," *Politics, Philosophy & Economics* 7(1) and Elizabeth Ashford (2003), "The Demandingness of Scanlon's Contractualism," *Ethics* 113(2).

burden of death is much more serious than the benefit of being able to travel more efficiently. But this doesn't seem right, given that the likelihood of the harm occurring is so low.

It is also implausible because disregarding risk means that "there is just as strong a reason for rejecting a principle permitting people to engage in behaviour that involves a small risk of bodily harm to others as for rejecting a principle that permits behaviour which is *certain* to cause harms of this same magnitude" (208, my emphasis). However, one would think that there should be less objection to the former principle since the harm is much less likely to occur. What's the solution?

Scanlon doesn't think that discounting the harm by the likelihood of burdening *someone* is the right way to respond to the problem. The example he gives to illustrate this point is a medical experiment that will subject a handful of people to painful and dangerous medical experiments for the benefit of a much larger number. If the weight of the burden imposed on these people is sharply discounted because only a small fraction of the population is affected (and therefore the risk to any particular person is so small), the medical experiment proposal could not be reasonably rejected. But Scanlon, as a contractualist, wants to keep open the possibility that the proposal could be reasonably rejected because of the severe burden it places on whoever ends up the unlucky subject of the experiment. At the same time, however, it also seems true that the "likelihood that a form of behaviour will lead to harm is an important factor in determining its permissibility" (209) and that it is assumed that the "only way to take this probability into account is as a factor that, in one way or another, diminishes the complaint of a person who suffers this harm" (209). The problem Scanlon has identified here is that it seems intuitively obvious that the probability of a harm occurring is relevant when determining whether a principle that imposes that risk of harm could be reasonably rejected. However, this also seems to diminish the complaint or seriousness of the harm on the person who ends up affected by it.

So how ought the probability of a harm occurring be incorporated into considerations of rejectability?

It seems to me that the uneasiness Scanlon has with the 'risk' in the medical experiment case is actually a recurrence or manifestation of his discomfort with aggregation. In explaining his rejection of interpersonal aggregation, Scanlon asks us to consider Jones, who works in the transmitter room for the television station broadcasting the World Cup final (235). Imagine that during the broadcast he is severely injured and the only way to relieve him of the pain he is experiencing is to turn off the match, which millions, maybe even billions, of people are watching. It is possible that the utility created from adding up the small enjoyment of each viewer would exceed the amount of pain Jones is experiencing. Scanlon thinks it is obvious that we ought to rescue Jones despite the fact that millions of people will miss out on watching the match because there are limits to what we can do to others in the name of the common good or utility. The small benefit accrued to each individual who would enjoy continuing coverage of the match cannot be aggregated to override the huge burden suffered by Jones if he is forced to remain in extreme pain for the duration of the match.

The same is true in the medical experiments case. There is only a risk to A (or any other person) because *someone must* have the burden imposed. Every person's 'risk', or chance of suffering the burden, is $1/n$, where n is the number of people who could be subject to the procedures. Rather than being a case of risk, it seems more clearly to be another example of how aggregated benefits cannot outweigh much more severe burdens incurred by individuals. Here the burden suffered by A in being forced to undergo the painful procedures cannot be outweighed by aggregating the benefit enjoyed by the majority as a result of the experiments. Scanlon does not need an account of permissible risk imposition in order to explain why the medical experiments are impermissible—he has already accounted for this with the individualist reasons restriction. The individualist reasons restriction precludes imposing a harm on someone for the sake of aggregated benefits to others—and therefore also precludes 'risk' imposition whenever it is guaranteed to be imposed on someone for the sake of benefiting others.

This means that actions that are 'risky' because they harm one person for the sake of benefiting others (thus only imposing a 'risk' on everyone insofar as there is a chance that *they* will be the person harmed) are rejectable on the grounds of aggregation rather than because they impose risk. They are rejectable precisely because they allow a (certain-to-happen) particular burden to be imposed on one person solely for the sake of an aggregated benefit for a larger group of other people. What remains to be seen is how we should deal with the more common kind of risks—where there is a chance that a burden will befall someone but it is neither necessary nor intended that it does, such as in the case of driving or air travel. These types of activities (e.g., driving), which benefit many people even though they risk severely burdening at least one person, are not a case of aggregated benefits to some outweighing the burden on others who are harmed as a result of the activity being permitted.

There are two key differences between the driving case and the medical experiments case. First, reaping the benefits of driving does not *require* someone to die, whereas the benefits of the medical experiment can be realized only if someone suffers extreme pain. Second, and related, if someone does die from themselves or others driving, it was by accident and not intended, as in the case of the medical experiments. Scanlon thinks that the second point is especially important. He believes that our assessment of the medical experiments case would be different if the harm in question were inflicted on people by accident, that is, if it "occurs despite the fact that reasonable precautions have been taken," rather than on particular people directly (209). The difference in this case does not have to do with the actual harm since in both cases it is the same. Rather, it is the behaviour of the agent that matters—we can accept a prohibition on intentionally inflicting serious harm but not on avoiding all behaviour that could potentially lead to the same harm.

This focus on the intentions and behaviours of the agent takes us to a distinction that several commentators have noted: *ex post* versus *ex ante* contractualist justifications of risk imposition. *Ex post* contractualism is the view that we should evaluate what is reasonable in light of the actual outcomes of the act or principle in question. In *ex ante* contractualism, only the expected outcomes count as grounds for objection.[2] In this latter way of reasoning, we consider the information available to the agents at the time of acting and what they can reasonably expect to happen given the information that is commonly available to a person in that situation. Most scholars agree that although there are places in *What We Owe to Each Other* where it appears that Scanlon is adopting an *ex post* perspective, contractualism is best understood *ex ante*. This is because contractualism, unlike Rawls' theory, allows real information to be made available to the actor. This means that agents are not deprived of knowledge of their circumstances, but they are also not furnished with information that they could not possibly know at the time of acting. James Lenman makes this point clearly:

> The primary foci of moral evaluation are actions, and actions are properly morally evaluated from the perspective of all affected parties to be sure, but always relative to an epistemic perspective available to the agent at the time of the action, not an epistemically privileged perspective from which outcomes are transparent. I have no complaint against your action if, at the time you acted, knowing what you could reasonably be expected then to know, I should reasonably have conceded that your action was acceptable.[3]

---

[2] Aaron James (2012), "Contractualism's (Not So) Slippery Slope," *Legal Theory* 18(3): 266.
[3] Lenman, "Contractualism and Risk Imposition": 115.

What this means for our purposes is that in considering how much risk we can impose on others, we consider only expected benefits or harms. So in the case of driving, we consider the likelihood of a car crashing and killing bystanders or passengers. Then, when determining *ex ante* whether the principle is rejectable or not, we would not compare death to the convenience of driving. Rather, we would consider the *risk* of death to the convenience of driving. Since the risk to each person is so slight, no one would have a reasonable objection to others driving as long as all reasonable precautions have been taken to reduce the risk. The precautions we are reasonably required to take will depend on the likelihood of the harm occurring:

> Our idea of 'reasonable precautions' defines the level of care that we think can be demanded: a principle that demanded more than this would be too confining, and could reasonably be rejected on that ground. (209)

If the likelihood of being killed in a car crash is only 0.01%, we may not need to take any special precautions at all. On the other hand, if it is higher, we may be required to take further precautions such as additional license requirements and limits on alcohol consumption and speed—in fact, all precautions that are routinely taken as a matter of course around the world. If a person is killed by a driver despite the relevant precautions having been taken, they would not have a reasonable objection to the principle that allowed driving since the principle was *ex ante* non-rejectable.

Ultimately, we focus on the actions we take *ex ante* rather than only on *ex post* outcomes. To do this we must take the probability of a harm occurring and the seriousness of the potential harm into account in deciding what precautions are reasonably required. In so doing we are also balancing the burdens that would be borne by taking those precautions. We find what is reasonable at the point at which those burdens are balanced by the probability and seriousness of the potential harm. If reasonable precautions were taken and a risk materialized and burdened a particular person, that person could not claim to have been wronged because the risk was not wrongfully imposed, as the principle permitting it was not *ex ante* reasonably rejectable.

Back to the Future

In the case of risky procreative decisions, we need to think about the perspective of the prospective parent and what they can reasonably be expected to know and do. The potential outcome for the child is important, but so is the likelihood of that outcome coming to fruition. In the case of uncertain outcomes, the precautions required to permissibly create a child will increase as the probability of a bad outcome increases and the worse the expected outcome is.

Earlier (Chapter 4), I discussed situations in which we were determining the permissibility of having a child with varying degrees of impairment or enhancement and argued that the worse the expected quality of life for the child, the stronger the reasons needed to justify the creation of the child. Now we need to hold the expected quality of life constant but allow the chances of it occurring to vary. Imagine two people have a chance of (separately) creating a child with a very bad life. Parent A has a 5% chance of creating a child with disease X, and parent B has a 75% chance of creating a child with disease X. The potential low quality of life (if it occurs) for the child is the same in both scenarios, but the likelihood of the child having that low quality of life is different. I believe in situations like this, a principle such as the following would be non-rejectable:

> *Reasonable Risk*: A person must take the precautions to avoid creating a child with a very bad life that are proportionate to the probability of creating such a child.

What this means is that parent A may be required to make some minor sacrifices in order to take precautions against their child developing disease X. Perhaps he or she ought to investigate certain lifestyle choices that could minimize the child's chances even further. On the other hand, much more would be required of parent B. He or she may be morally obligated to go through IVF treatments or pre-implantation genetic diagnosis (for example) in order to test for disease X and select an embryo that doesn't have it. In either case, if the child were ultimately born with a very bad life, he could not reasonably reject the principle that permitted the mother to conceive, given that she took the precautions that were reasonable relative to the probability of the bad outcome coming to fruition.

For an example of how the principle might work in practice, consider Tay-Sachs disease, a debilitating condition that is present at birth and fatal within three to five years. The HEXA gene mutation that causes the disease is quite rare in the general population (1 in 300, or 0.3%).[4] The average person knows that their chances of creating a child with the disease is extremely low and therefore is not required to take any special steps to prevent it. However, very specific communities including Ashkenazi Jews, Louisiana residents of French Canadian heritage, and the Pennsylvania Amish carry the mutation at much higher frequencies, as high as 3–4% in the Ashkenazi population.[5] People with these backgrounds or with family members who were born with the disease know their chance of carrying the mutation is substantially higher than average and would have more responsibility to take precautions such as genetic testing of themselves and their partners or pre-implantation embryonic testing.[6] In fact, the Jewish community seems to follow something like this principle. The organization Dor Yeshorim offers genetic screening to Jewish children, who are

---

[4] National Organization for Rare Diseases, "Tay Sachs Disease," https://rarediseases.org/rare-diseases/tay-sachs-disease/ (accessed June 14, 2022).
[5] National Tay-Sachs & Allied Diseases Association, "Tay-Sachs Disease," http://www.tay-sachs.org/taysachs_disease.php (accessed June 14, 2022).
[6] Dor Yeshorim Centre for Jewish Genetics, https://www.jewishgenetics.org/dor-yeshorim (accessed June 14, 2022).

then issued with a personal identification number (PIN). Later in life when a couple meets and considers a relationship, each enters their PIN in the organization's database and are informed of whether they both carry the gene. If they do, they are advised not to pursue the relationship, as the chance of both parties passing on the gene and having a child with Tay-Sachs disease is 25%. If they do choose to continue the relationship, they have the genetic information they need to make informed decisions about their procreative choices in light of the high chance of conceiving a child with Tay-Sachs disease. In this case, the precautions that are taken by Ashkenazi Jews are not unreasonable relative to the respective risk of creating a child with a very bad life, as they are not overly intrusive or restrictive.

We now have two principles pertaining to the creation of children with bad lives—*Bad Lives* and *Reasonable Risk*—and it could be asked how the two intersect with each other. The answer is that they apply in different contexts. *Bad Lives* is the principle that guides us when we know that if we procreate under these conditions, we will create a child with a very bad life. It tells when that would be permissible. *Reasonable Risk* guides us when we are not certain of the outcome and helps us determine what precautions we must take when procreating under conditions of uncertainty. For this reason, in the world as it stands now, *Reasonable Risk* would be the principle that guides most people in their procreative decisions since most people do not have extensive knowledge of their own propensities to pass along certain diseases or disabilities and do not engage in IVF therapies. However, more and more people are moving towards knowing more about themselves and their potential children. Companies like 23andme offer genetic mapping for about US$100.[7] In just a few weeks an individual can find out their

---

[7] In addition to telling you your predisposition to conditions like Alzheimer's disease, 23andme (https://www.23andme.com/) will also tell you the arguably more important fact of whether you are likely to be disturbed by other people's chewing or prone to sneeze in sunlight.

genetic predispositions to conditions like early-onset Alzheimer's disease and Huntington's disease, and, crucially, the likelihood of passing these genes on to children.[8] Similarly, many couples could choose to undertake IVF therapy not only as a way of enabling reproduction for otherwise infertile couples but also to have the opportunity for preimplantation genetic screening and selection. As the world changes, it is possible that *Bad Lives* and *Good Lives* will become the more commonly applicable principles.

What Do Future People Need?

Now, for a different kind of imperfect knowledge, I will examine two related questions that both spring from the fact that some generations will live in the very distant future. First, what types of things must we leave in order to satisfy our obligations to future people, and second, what effect do our epistemic limitations have on our obligations?

I argued in Chapter 3 that it is important to ensure that future generations' basic needs are met so that they have the opportunity to live sufficiently good lives. To begin with the first question, there are things that will always be required for people to lead sufficiently good lives. For now I will bracket the second question and assume that we can predict what those things are. Examples could include nutritious food, shelter, clean water, a good environment, and so on. It is important to realize that although these are all essential aspects of decent lives, in some cases we are not actually leaving future generations with these things. Sometimes we are: for example, when we mitigate climate change, we provide future generations

---

[8] Invitae offers testing for 264 genetic conditions for just US$150, and CNN Money expects that full genome mapping will soon be available for as little as US$100. See Invitae, "Deeper Genetic Insights," https://invitae.com/en/test-catalog/; Eilene Zimmerman, "The Race to a $100 Genome," CNN Money, June 25, 2013, http://money.cnn.com/2013/06/25/technology/enterprise/low-cost-genome-sequencing/.

with a good environment. Many times, however, what we are providing them with are the satisfiers of these needs. We do not, for example, leave behind cows or milk for food, or enough houses for every person who will ever exist to live in. Rather, we leave arable land for farming, and the resources (e.g., sustainable forests) for building accommodation. Even in the case of non-renewable natural resources, the resources themselves may not necessarily be a basic need but rather may be satisfiers of basic needs (e.g., iron ore is the satisfier used to produce the steel for housing, which is the basic need). Even in cases where the resource is also the basic need, we can still consider it as a simply more direct satisfier. Clean water satisfies the basic need for clean water simply by existing, and steel (from iron ore) satisfies the need for housing by being used in buildings. There is an extra step in the case of steel, but the structure is the same. It is clear then that in the case of future generations, what we are distributing are the satisfiers of basic needs.

These satisfiers could take one of two forms. They could be either direct resources, like oil and iron ore, or substitutions, like technology. To see how a substitution would work, consider the case of Norway's oil fund. In 1990 the government of Norway decided to put the income from the country's petroleum industry into a pension fund. The proceeds from oil have been invested and have grown significantly since the fund's establishment, and as of early 2023 the fund was worth almost US$1.3 trillion.[9] In this way Norway has decided to use its oil reserves rather than saving them for the future; however, the country is leaving future people with significant wealth in the form of the oil fund. The idea is that Norway has substituted monetary wealth for natural resource wealth: "One day the oil will run out, but the return on the fund will continue to benefit the Norwegian population."[10] There is a debate

---

[9] Norges Bank Investment Management, http://www.nbim.no (accessed February 14, 2023).
[10] Norges Bank Investment Management, "The Fund," http://www.nbim.no/en/the-fund/ (accessed February 14, 2023).

within the sustainability literature about whether substitutions are permissible, with 'weak sustainability' theorists saying yes and 'strong sustainability' theorists disagreeing.[11] Because my view is that we ought to leave future generations with the *opportunity* for living sufficiently good lives, I think it is unimportant what form the satisfiers/resources we leave them take. Thus, substitutions would also be valid ways to meet our intergenerational obligations.

Let us now un-bracket and address the epistemic problem. Distant generations may have different ways of life, technologies, and cultural norms than we do. What is important or necessary for our sufficiency may not be for them, and vice versa. How can we leave them enough satisfiers when we have only a limited idea of what 'enough' will be for them? Here I will invoke the 'ought implies can' provision: we cannot be morally required to do something we are not able to do. Likewise, if we cannot know precisely how many resources people in the future will need in order to lead sufficiently good lives, we are not morally derelict if we do not end up leaving them with enough despite our best efforts and intentions.

This brings us back to the earlier discussion of permissible risk imposition. As was the case there, what is important is that, as agents acting *ex ante*, we make assessments about what the probabilities are of different scenarios occurring and take reasonable precautions—that is, precautions that are commensurate with the severity and probability of the potential risk. This means that we are not required to be excessively risk-averse and conserve everything we have just in case future people require a lot more resources to have the opportunity for sufficiently good lives. Instead, we are required to make an assessment of the probable quantity and quality of resources future people will need to have this opportunity and use that assessment as the basis for our conservation decisions. What is key is that any lack of knowledge does not absolve us of

---

[11] Eric Neumayer (2003), *Weak Versus Strong Sustainability: Exploring the Limits of Two Opposing Paradigms*, 2nd ed. (Cheltenham: Edward Elgar).

our duty to leave them with enough. Perhaps the duty should be more precisely stated as an obligation to make a good-faith effort to leave future generations with enough satisfiers to have the opportunity to lead sufficiently good lives, but this is a quite cumbersome phrasing.

How to Factor in Numbers of Future Generations

Unless there is an unexpected disaster, there will be a lot of future people, more than are currently alive today. If current generations are required to provide enough resources for all of these future people to live sufficiently good lives, it would seem that it would require current people to use no resources at all. If there is x quantity of resources available in the world and future generations will need all x of them due to their sheer numbers, then the current generation would not be permitted to use *any* of them. For one thing, it seems unfair to require one generation to provide for all subsequent generations, but it would also have the odd implication that no generation could ever be permitted to use any resources.

Assume discrete and consecutive generations: $G_w, G_x, G_y \ldots G_n$. When G_w is the current generation they are not permitted to use any resources because doing so would mean that not every future generation would lead sufficiently good lives. When G_x is the current generation, they too are not permitted to use any resources because doing so would mean that the very numerous generations that follow them would not be able to live sufficiently good lives, and so on ad infinitum. No one is ever able to realize sufficiently good lives in this scenario, due to the risk of future generations being unable to as well. A paradoxical situation arises in which a principle intended to provide sufficiency for the future in fact provides sufficiency for no one (including the future).

However, as I said earlier, the current generation can prioritize their own sufficiency when ensuring that future generations have sufficiency would require so much sacrifice of the current generation that they are not able to meet sufficiency themselves. Assume for the sake of argument that Generations W, X, and Y cannot meet sufficiency for themselves if they are not permitted to use any resources. In that case their obligation to provide sufficiency for the future is nullified and they are permitted to use these resources. However, this would essentially mean that there is no obligation on the part of these generations to save anything; if true, this brings into question the value of the *Sufficient Resources* principle in the first place. If it is impossible to satisfy the principle, what is the point of having it?

I believe that distinguishing between positive and negative duties helps address the problem. Each generation has a negative duty to all succeeding generations not to act in ways that those later generations could reasonably reject. This means that we may still have negative duties not to create terrible harms for people throughout time and not to act in ways that make it impossible for them to enjoy sufficiently good lives. For example, we should not leave Parfitian time bombs for children to come across in 200 years' time (unmitigated climate change might seem, to some, to be an example of a metaphorical 'time bomb'). At the same time, we might also say that it is not the case that each generation has a positive duty to all future generations to conserve and invest such that the later generations have the opportunity for sufficiently good lives.

There are two reasons the positive duty to provide for every future generation is not borne by a given current generation. First, the duty-bearers for Generation Z's standard of living can only include those who could act in ways likely to benefit or burden Generation Z—again, because of the 'ought implies can' proviso. A generation alive now could not be expected to have a positive duty to those living in 500 years' time because so much will happen between now and then that positive actions taken now will make little difference to the standard of life in 2515. However, the current generation can have a material impact on the lives of those living in, say, 80 years' time.

Second, if the world economy continues to grow as expected, it would be unfair to make the current generation conserve everything they can for those living in 2515 when the former would be much poorer than the latter.[12] However, those people living in 2415 (for example) could be expected to have a positive duty to assist.

These two criteria—who is likely to positively affect a generation and whom it would be fair to ask to conserve for a generation—can give reasons as to why a generation owes positive duties to only some succeeding generations.

---

[12] If economic growth does not continue as projected, currently existing people may not be significantly poorer than those living in 2515. However, in that case, the first point (ability to positively assist) is still relevant.

7
What *Do* We Owe to Future People?

So far I have said a lot about intergenerational ethical principles in the abstract, and now I want to answer the book's titular question more directly. I can't hope to address what we ought to do with respect to each of our choices that might affect future people, but I do want to explore at least some of the implications of the principles that I have argued for.

Procreating When You're...

In Chapter 4 I defended the following principle:

> *Bad Lives:* It is impermissible to create a child who will have an insufficiently good life when it would take only a small or moderate sacrifice for the parent(s) to prevent it.

Following this principle has a number of interesting implications in different procreative scenarios. It's obvious that a lot of different factors affect whether or not a child will have a sufficiently good life. Some of these are purely a matter of biological or genetic chance (chromosomal abnormalities, randomly developing cancer), but others are down to parental choice, background, or societal context (which may or may not be within the parents' control).

... Old, Unhappy, or Oppressed

Let's start with parents' choices. While most women are confined by nature to having children before the age of about 45 (give or take), some men choose to have children when they are much older. Life expectancy for males in developed countries is currently between 76 and 80 years old. This means that if a man fathers a child after about 60 years of age, there is a high probability he will die before his child becomes an adult. He will probably miss his child's high school graduation and wedding and the birth of his grandchildren. But this story is not really about what the father will miss; it's about his child. The child will lose her father before she is an adult herself, and a good proportion of her childhood may be spent caring for and/or worrying about her aging father. She will not have his emotional or financial support during her transition to adulthood, which is becoming later and later.[1]

Parents may also choose to have children in already poor familial situations—to save an ailing marriage, for example. Children born into these conditions may suffer through parental arguments, marital breakup, and the economic and emotional impact of divorce and subsequently being raised in a single-parent home. These are all negative impacts on the child, but unlikely to mean that she has an insufficiently good life, so not precluded by the *Bad Lives* principle. However, the *Good Lives* principle requires us to create the best possible child if we can do so at minimal sacrifice.

Whether or not this affects our older father depends on a number of factors. If he knows he wants two children (for example) and is delaying having them for trivial reasons like wanting more time to spend with his friends at the bar, then he has violated *Good Lives*. But if he is waiting because he has not met the right partner, he

---

[1] Judith G. Dey and Charles R. Pierret (2014), "Independence for Young Millennials: Moving Out and Boomeranging Back," *Monthly Labor Review*, U.S. Bureau of Labor Statistics.

doesn't act wrongly because it would be a significant sacrifice to require him to have children with the wrong person simply to make the children better off by virtue of having a younger father (it's also arguable whether the children would be better off since there will be downsides to having unhappy parents). In general, though, while it might be better for men to have children earlier in life, or for people to wait until their relationship is strong, it's unlikely that a child born into these situations has reason to object to their parents' choices if they still have sufficiently good lives and being made even better off would have required significant sacrifice.

Some might also worry that my account means that it would be wrong to have children who are members of oppressed groups (e.g., Black, female). It is undeniable that in countries such as the United States and Canada, being a member of one of these groups negatively affects your life prospects to different degrees. We are all too familiar with the depressing statistics that in the United States Black people and women are overrepresented in poverty and underrepresented in government and business. As unfortunate as it is that people may be disadvantaged due to no fault of their own, these disadvantages are not, I suspect, significant enough to make their lives insufficiently good, so there is no objection to procreating, even if the resulting Black or female children have lives that are less good than their white male counterparts.

One current exception to this could be the creation of girls in countries where it is very bad to be female. There is one country where women's oppression is particularly severe that immediately springs to mind: Afghanistan. In Afghanistan under the Taliban from 1996 until the US invasion in 2001,[2] women could not be educated past the age of eight, could not leave the house without a *mahram* (male relative), in most cases were banned from

---

[2] At the time of writing in early 2023, the Taliban has recently returned to power in Afghanistan. It remains to be seen exactly how many of these harsh laws will return, but it is very sadly looking increasingly likely that they will.

employment, could not access medical care (due to a lack of female doctors), were required to be fully covered by a burqa with only a mesh slit to see through, and were subject to forced marriage where they were entirely at the mercy of their husbands. With no recourse to divorce, Afghan women are regularly raped, beaten, and starved by their husbands. They were regularly flogged or executed for breaking the Taliban's harsh rules. Women without a *mahram* were effectively under house arrest.

In one respect it seems that bringing female children into this context would be wrong, as girls and women clearly did not live sufficiently good lives by any means. On the other hand, what would be the alternatives? Pregnant women in Afghanistan certainly weren't receiving ultrasounds to find out the sex of their babies, and even if they did, they would not have had access to abortion, even if they had wanted one. Nonetheless, let's assume these problems away for the moment. Is having an abortion a low to moderate sacrifice in order to prevent a girl being born into this insufficiently good life? Maybe, if done at the earliest stages of pregnancy. But there are other factors to consider. If it were wrong to have female children and everyone complied, there would only be boys born, massively shifting the gender balance of Afghan society, and likely making the situation for women even *worse*. Not only would women be outnumbered, but there would be men competing for them. When most 'commodities' are in short supply, the price or value usually goes up. With women, however, I suspect this would not be the case and that women would just be subjected to the same violence and control, but from multiple men instead of just one.

... Poor

It is a sad fact that in many parts of the world people live insufficiently good lives due to extreme poverty. Is it wrong to have children if you live in these kinds of conditions and any child you have will have an insufficiently good life? The answer to this depends on the 'moderate sacrifice' part of the *Bad Lives* principle. The places where people live in this kind of poverty are also places where it is not always easy to prevent pregnancy. Contraception may be difficult to obtain for geographical reasons (travel to get it is unaffordable) or for religious reasons, or the cost may just be prohibitively expensive. Any or all of these reasons might mean that preventing the creation of a person with a very bad life is much more than a moderate sacrifice and therefore not required. Furthermore, women in many patriarchal societies do not have the effective (and often also formal) freedom to decide when and if they want to conceive and more than 2.6 billion women live in countries where marital rape is explicitly legal.[3] I would not want to say that a woman in these conditions who has a child with an insufficiently good life has done something wrong, because the costs of avoiding pregnancy in that situation would be extreme—sometimes even death.

Even when avoiding pregnancy is possible at low to moderate sacrifice, it might nonetheless be permissible to procreate. If the only child you could have or adopt will live in extreme poverty such that they do not have a sufficiently good life, it may still be permissible because forgoing having a child at all is more than a moderate sacrifice. However, as I argued in Chapter 4, people may reasonably be limited in the number of children they can permissibly have once the good of childbirth/childrearing has been realised.

However, people who live in this kind of poverty in the developing world often rely on having large families to help on subsistence farms or to earn money to support the household. So there may still be significant sacrifices involved in not having more children. Not having a

---

[3] Marital rape is explicitly legal in at least 20 countries (for example, Tanzania, Ethiopia, and Yemen) and part of customary law or simply not criminalised in many more (for example, Afghanistan, Democratic Republic of the Congo, and India). Michelle J. Anderson (2016), "Marital Rape Laws Globally," in *Marital Rape: Consent, Marriage, and Social Change in Global Context*, ed. Kersti Yllo and M. Gabriella Torres (Oxford University Press).

large family might involve serious economic sacrifice. Whether this is true will depend on a particular person's situation. It would be wrong for parents who have easy access to contraceptives and no economic need for additional children to continue to procreate after having realised the good of procreation and parenting; however, I doubt if this is a very common scenario for people in these parts of the world.

One might point out that it is unfair that my theory limits poor people in their procreative choices but not rich people. I agree that it is unfair, but I don't see it as a problem particular to my account. It is essential to combat world poverty, among other things, because it limits choice and freedom. Poor people are limited in all sorts of ways that rich people are not; my account merely demonstrates that procreation is one of those ways. If anything, my conclusion should add weight to the importance of doing everything we can to ensure that no one needs to make these kinds of choices.

. . . Not Intending to Parent

Rivka Weinberg argues that parents need to have the intention to rear their children in order to permissibly create them. That rules out gamete donations and surrogacy. Unlike Weinberg, I don't think that you need to plan to rear the children you create in order to avoid wronging them, but I do think there is a question of who is the 'parent' and therefore responsible for ensuring that the resulting children have sufficiently good lives.

Many people use gamete donation or surrogates to procreate. Homosexual couples need either a sperm or egg donor, and male homosexual couples also need a woman to act as a gestational surrogate as well. Many heterosexual couples find that one partner's sperm or eggs are defective in some way and require a donor, and single women having children on their own through sperm donation are an increasingly common phenomenon. The quality of life a person has will be affected by nature and nurture, so it seems that anyone involved in the decision to create a child is subject to the principles I've outlined, and this includes gamete donors and women acting as gestational surrogates.

Does the fact that a child is conceived from donated gametes affect the likelihood of them having a sufficiently good life? It's possible. Some argue that not knowing your biological roots is bad for a child, and that knowing 'where you come from' is essential to your well-being. Furthermore, there is evidence that even newborn babies experience trauma when separated from their gestational mother (even when the gestational mother is not the baby's genetic mother).[4] There is also some (albeit limited) evidence of less positive mother-child interaction in families created through surrogacy with egg donation than in families that conceived naturally.[5] Although more research needs to be done, it does seem unlikely that any negative effects of being donor-conceived or the child of a surrogate will be significant enough to render a child's life insufficiently good. Given that, the principle of *Good Lives* applies. The child is expected to have at least a sufficiently good life, but that does not mean our job is done. Donors and surrogates can reasonably be expected to create the best possible child, so long as it takes little sacrifice. Allowing one's basic identity and medical information to be known by the child, for example, is not a great sacrifice, yet it may significantly improve the child's life, so it is morally required.

... Trying to Save Another Child

'Saviour siblings' are children who are created with the intention of donating cord blood to an existing child who is sick with certain forms

---

[4] Marcus Agnafors (2014), "The Harm Argument Against Surrogacy Revisited: Two Versions Not to Forget," *Medicine, Health Care and Philosophy* 17.

[5] Susan Golombok et al. (2011), "Families Created Through Surrogacy: Mother-Child Relationships and Children's Psychological Adjustment at Age 7," *Developmental Psychology* 47(6).

of blood diseases such as leukaemia and aplastic anaemia. The parents go through in vitro fertilization and pre-implantation genetic diagnosis of the embryo in order to select one that is a match for the existing ill child. They then go through pregnancy and birth as normal, and after the placenta is delivered, the cord blood is collected and transplanted to the ill child. None of this is painful or harmful to the newborn baby.

Some people, including philosophers, are uncomfortable with the idea of saviour siblings because they worry that the child is being treated merely as a means and the child is harmed in being created for this purpose. While I think these worries are understandable, they are also misguided. On the view I have presented in this book, saviour siblings will usually be permissible. The people affected by a principle permitting saviour siblings are the parents, who will lose their sick child if not permitted to create a matching child; the child who will die; and of course the saviour sibling themselves. It seems fairly clear that neither the parents nor the sick child would have reason to reject a principle allowing them to create a saviour sibling because they only stand to gain from it.

The only real objection might come from the saviour sibling themselves. What could their objections be? If they are created and their parents treat them badly (because they never *really* wanted them in the first place), they would have a strong objection. But if they are created and their parents treat them just as well as, if not better than, than the existing child, what objection could they have? Perhaps they might say, "I object to this principle because you created me as a means to some end and not for my own sake." I have two responses to this.

First, as I have argued elsewhere with Caleb Althorpe, almost all reasons for procreation are instrumental—to enjoy the goods of parenting, to create companions for existing children, to have someone to take care of you in old age, to fulfil religious obligations, and so on.[6] Almost no one creates children for the purpose of

---

[6] Caleb Althorpe and Elizabeth Finneron-Burns (forthcoming), "Are Saviour Siblings a Special Case in Procreative Ethics?" *Journal of Ethics and Social Philosophy*.

giving a child the opportunity to exist. Second, even if a person did have that last motivation, it's not clear that it is a coherent one. It is not possible to create someone for their own sake, since they do not exist at the time you make the decision to create them.[7]

So, assuming that the parents give the saviour sibling a sufficiently good life, there is no real objection, and only reasons in favour. However, there would be an objection if once the child is created the parents treat the saviour sibling as inferior to the older child. Althorpe and I have argued that this is unlikely for several reasons;[8] however, were it to happen, the saviour child would have an objection not to their creation itself, but to any principle allowing parents to arbitrarily treat one of their children better than another.

Climate Policy

The Intergovernmental Panel on Climate Change's (IPCC) Sixth Assessment Report (AR6) suggests that in the mid- to long term (20–80 years), climate change will, among other things, undermine food security and nutrition in developing parts of the world (sub-Saharan Africa, South Asia, Central America, and South America), leading to malnutrition. It will also increase poor health and premature death from heatwaves, floods, and water-borne, food-borne, and vector-borne diseases, in particular from dengue fever, which is expected to spread geographically and put additional billions of people at risk by the end of the century.[9] The AR6 also expects that mental health challenges (e.g., anxiety and stress) will increase around the world. By this point any reasonable person understands

---

[7] Claudia Mills (2005), "Are There Morally Problematic Reasons for Having Children?," *Philosophy & Public Policy Quarterly* 25(4).

[8] Althorpe and Finneron-Burns (forthcoming), "Are Saviour Siblings a Special Case in Procreative Ethics?"

[9] Intergovernmental Panel on Climate Change (2022), "Climate Change 2022: Impacts, Adaptation, and Vulnerability": 15.

that climate change has the potential to have a significant impact on future people. I say "potential" not because climate change may not actually cause these harms, but because it is still possible to prevent many of them.[10] Whether or not this happens is up to us.

There is some debate among climate ethicists, scientists, and economists about what the goal for climate mitigation should be— 2°C above pre-industrial temperatures, 1.5°C, etc.[11] I am (clearly) neither a climate scientist nor an economist, but since different temperature increases are associated with different outcomes for future people, it seems that what we can do is figure out what an ethical outcome would be and work backwards to determine how much/whether mitigation is required.

The view I have defended is that, in the first instance, we owe it to future people to provide them with the opportunity for a sufficiently good life, unless it would take more than a moderate sacrifice to do so. Clearly things like proper nutrition and good health (including mental health) are part of whether a person's life is sufficiently good. The dangers of more than a 2°C temperature rise listed above seem clearly to jeopardize future people's opportunity to enjoy sufficiently good lives. So it would be wrong to allow temperatures to rise above 2°C unless it would take significant sacrifice to prevent it. What kinds of sacrifices might be required?

The sacrifices involved can be viewed at both the collective (government) and individual levels. It seems clear that governments could and should be doing a lot more to mitigate climate change with only small cost/sacrifice. For example, they could tax fossil fuel companies, incentivise green companies, invest in green energy and technological development, and develop transport policies and urban planning that reduce the need for cars.

---

[10] Unfortunately, previous emissions and a failure to mitigate up to this point mean that some harms are inevitable.
[11] Simon Caney (2021), "Climate Justice," *The Stanford Encyclopedia of Philosophy*, ed. Edward N. Zalta (Stanford University Press).

On an individual level, perhaps the most significant thing a person could do would be to lobby/pressure the government to take the necessary actions listed above. Lobbying can be as simple as writing letters to lawmakers, and it seems that people are morally obligated to do so up to the point where the time involved becomes more than a moderate sacrifice.

Other than influencing government actions, the following four actions have been shown to be most effective on the individual level: having one fewer child (saves 58.6 tonnes of CO_2/year), living car-free (2.4 tonnes/year), avoiding air travel (1.6 tonnes/trip), and adopting a plant-based diet (0.8 tonnes/year).[12] I've already argued that if you already have a child, then not having another one is not a serious sacrifice. If you do *not* already have a child, then it is probably permissible to have one even though it may contribute to warming (depending on whether others also follow the principle). Living car-free and avoiding air travel will be small sacrifices for some but more than moderate for others. A person who lives in a compact European city with good public transit options and whose family all live nearby, for example, may find this easy. On the other hand, someone living in a sprawling North American city with poor public transit options, or someone whose immediate family lives overseas, will not. It would be a great sacrifice not to have a car somewhere where it took several hours each way to get to work on public transit or to the grocery store to buy food (which would need to be done multiple times a week given that one would be limited in how much they could buy by how much they could carry). Similarly, not being able to visit with your close family who lives overseas would be significant, especially for important events like babies being born, weddings, caring for sick relatives, saying goodbye to close family members before they die, and funerals.

---

[12] Seth Wynes and Kimberly A. Nicholas (2017), "The Climate Mitigation Gap: Education and Government Recommendations Miss the Most Effective Individual Actions," *Environmental Research Letters* 12.

Depriving people of these opportunities would be a serious sacrifice. On the other hand, for most of us, giving up farmed meat would not be (and I *love* a good steak).

Even though some people may not be required to give up their cars or air travel, that isn't necessarily the end of the story. They would still be required not to drive when reasonable alternatives are available, and to limit their trips where possible—i.e., they may permissibly use them when not using them would be an undue sacrifice. Similarly with air travel, it would only be permissible to fly for important reasons, and not just for fun. Tourism and vacations are good for a person's understanding of the world, other cultures, and mental health. Following the principle might mean that we ought to seek out travel and vacation opportunities that do not require flying, or limit our discretionary air travel to once a decade (for example) instead of once a year. Essentially, whenever not travelling by air becomes more than a moderate sacrifice, we can permissibly do it.

Imagine that we follow these principles and limit warming such that future people have (just) sufficiently good lives. Are we required to do even more? This is where the *Additional Resources* principle would kick in. We would still be required to mitigate, but only if the sacrifices were minimal. At this point, people who are ambivalent about meat should give it up, but those who are mad about meat wouldn't have to. We should still take the bus if it takes the same amount of time as driving, even if it's a little less comfortable or convenient, but not if it's raining and we would get soaked. And if a British person is deciding between a wine-tasting vacation to South Africa and one to Italy, with only the desire for good wine driving the decision, they should go to Italy (oh, to have that choice!).[13]

---

[13] I write this in the depths of a Canadian winter during a pandemic, so this is one decision I wish I had to make.

Population Policies

Governments around the world commonly adopt pro- and anti-natalist policies (though not usually at the same time!). Everyone knows about China's anti-natalist one-child policy that was in place from 1980 until it was scrapped in 2016. This was a particularly severe way to discourage population growth, but states also have less harsh tools at their disposal. In the United Kingdom a couple can only receive certain welfare benefits for their first two children (with limited exceptions including children born from rape), and Singapore's former "Stop at Two" campaign did not allow maternity leave for third and subsequent babies. There are also many governments around the world, China now included, who are actually trying to *encourage* population growth. States use tax credits, direct payments, free childcare, and fully paid extended parental leaves to encourage people to have more children.

My analysis suggests that many of these policies will be permissible. In terms of anti-natalist policies, the children who will never be born as a result have no claims, but the parents who would otherwise have had more children do. So too do those children who will be born into a smaller population than they would have been in the absence of the anti-natalist policy. If the burden imposed on a parent due to a particular anti-natalist policy is sufficiently great, then perhaps they could reasonably reject it. From the parents' perspectives, a legal one-child policy like China's may be rejectable if it seriously interferes with the ability of a family to live their lives autonomously. Although parents will have enjoyed the benefits of parenting (once they have their allotted child), there may be other burdens like not having support in old age. Similarly, the children who are born may object to the principle because they are deprived of siblings to help them care for aging parents. On the other hand, the children may also benefit if the smaller population they're born into enjoys a higher quality of life than it would have with unrestricted population growth. Furthermore, anti-natalist policies that penalise creating additional children may perpetuate social inequalities, particularly for women. If a policy like Singapore's eliminates maternity leave, then women are the ones who will bear the full brunt of the policy, not men. Additionally, as I have already noted, women do not always have the ability to choose how many children they have. In extremely patriarchal societies they may have no power over this whatsoever, but even in developed liberal countries, women may be raped, lack access to reliable birth control and abortion, or have religious/moral convictions that preclude abortion. This means that black-and-white policies like "one child no matter what" are likely rejectable, whereas nudging policies that take into account the context and circumstances of that society may not be.

What about pro-natalist policies? Historically, pro-natalist policies have never been as extreme as anti-natalist ones. They usually just try to make childbearing and childrearing more financially viable for families, rather than forcing procreation. Providing incentives to couples to have more children does not seem to create many objections, so long as the population size that will result is still a permissible one. Encouraging procreation such that the children who will exist will have less than sufficiently good lives would be wrong because those children could reject the policy. If, on the other hand, the population were extremely large and someone wanted to make it even larger for some selfish reason, regardless of the quality of life the people would have, any principle allowing these pro-natalist incentives would be wrong.

Whether a particular pro- or anti-natalist principle is rejectable or not will depend on factors specific to the context in which it is proposed. So, rather than attempt to say which specific policies are justifiable and which are not, my point here is just that some pro- and anti-natalist policies to encourage and stanch population growth, respectively, are in principle permissible.

Existential Risk and Longtermism

Scientists agree that human extinction is virtually guaranteed to happen eventually. Nonetheless, many people dedicate their lives to researching ways to postpone this eventuality for as long as possible. I argued in Chapter 5 that human extinction would not be *per se* bad or wrong but that the way it comes about could be wrong if it causes involuntary premature death or pain (physical or psychological). What this means is that the bad/wrong of human extinction is not lessened by it happening farther in the future. Put another way, it's not better for human extinction to happen later rather than sooner. If extinction comes about voluntarily, then it makes no difference whether we make that decision today or in thousands of years. Similarly, if it is *not* voluntary, the pain that will be experienced by the people who live at the time is not made better by the fact that it won't happen until the distant future.

This suggests that research on existential risk should be focused not necessarily on reducing the risk of extinction itself, but on reducing the harm, pain, and suffering of the people who will exist when it happens. This may sound defeatist or plainly wrong to some people. But if human extinction really is inevitable, seeking to put it off as long as possible is saying to future people: 'I didn't want my generation or those I care about to be the ones to suffer the pain of extinction occurring, so I did everything I could to make sure you experienced it instead.' I don't for a moment think that researchers of existential risk have anything but the most honourable intentions, but this is an implication of the argument. Perhaps research into existential risk will mean that extinction is no longer inevitable. That would be a very good result, but only because it means no one will have to suffer the harms of extinction occurring. At a minimum, research into existential risk should be expanded to include trying to minimize the harmful effects extinction will have on the people who exist when it happens.

Closely related to existential risk is the relatively new philosophy of 'longtermism'. The basic premise of longtermism is that future people matter just as much as current people, so we "ought to be concerned with ensuring that the far future goes well."[14] Furthermore, the expected number of future lives is *vast*.[15] Consequently, if our goal is to do the most good, then the key moral priority for us should be shaping the far future by preventing premature human extinction for as long as possible and developing artificial superintelligence, even if this comes at the expense of current people.

I agree, of course, with the basic premise that future people matter. However, I do not believe that contractualism, in its intact form, is fundamentally compatible with longtermism. I have already discussed human extinction and existential risk mitigation specifically, but there are also other reasons contractualists should reject this philosophy. For one thing, the individual reasons restriction precludes aggregating future people's claims in the way longtermists suggest. The fact that there will be significantly more future people than current people is not a reason to prioritise their interests. For another, as I have argued throughout, there is no reason per se for a contractualist to be concerned with ensuring that humanity continues for as long as possible, whether that be on Earth, in space, or as digital minds. In a working paper, Owen Clifton and Rahul Kumar agree, arguing that in order for a contractualist to have a path to endorsing strong longtermism, they would have to give up either the individualist restriction or the personal reasons restriction.[16] As I and others have argued, there are good reasons to preserve these restrictions on reasons, and contractualists can support obligations to future generations even with them in place.

---

[14] Hilary Greaves and William MacAskill (2021), "The Case for Strong Longtermism," Global Priorities Institute Working Paper, University of Oxford: 1.

[15] Greaves and MacAskill (2021): 9. Greaves and MacAskill estimate the number of future people to be at least 10^{24}. This figure assumes a non-negligible probability that humans will expand into space and/or develop digital intelligence.

[16] Owen Clifton and Rahul Kumar (in preparation), "Should Contractualists Be Longtermists?"

8
Conclusion

Intersecting Principles

The arguments I've made in this book all intersect with each other in interesting and complicated ways. First, although we have a principle guiding population size, it is individuals who are ultimately the people who create a population through procreation. The balance of reasons at play in an individual's decision about whether or not to have a child (whether the child will have a sufficiently good life, for example) are intricately tied up with the size of the population. If the population is very large such that there is overcrowding (for example), the child might not have a sufficiently good life, which would provide the parent with a strong reason not to create the child.

Second, the population sizes that are permissible will also affect the permissibility of procreation. Suppose it turned out that a particular population size (population A) could only be brought about through rejectable principles and it would therefore be wrong to create population A. Imagine also that were Alice to have a child, that child would be the person who made population A exist. The fact that it would be wrong to create population A provides Alice with a reason not to procreate, and that reason must be balanced against the reasons she has to want to have a child.

Third, the resources available to a particular generation will affect the permissibility of an individual procreative decision and/ or a given population size. If resources are limited, this will affect the opportunity a child will have to enjoy a sufficiently good life, which could provide a reason to the parent not to have the child. If that reason is stronger than the other reasons that are present, it could be wrong for the parent to procreate, and this would be due to the availability of resources, rather than to anything the individual parent has done or not done.

Population size and resource distribution are even more closely related. A generation's size will affect how many resources are necessary for current people to leave for the future. The greater the population, presumably, the more resources that generation will need in order to have the opportunity to live sufficiently good lives, and vice versa. From the other perspective, the number of resources that a generation has available to them will affect the permissibility of a particular population size. Permissible population sizes are determined by the balance of reasons, and the ability of a particular generation to have the opportunity for sufficiently good lives is a very strong reason. If resources are too scarce to provide this opportunity at a particular population size, that population size could be reasonably rejected. Thus, decisions about how many resources need to be left for the future cannot be separated from a discussion about the optimal population size of the next generation(s).

The interrelated nature of these principles may seem to muddy the waters. What seemed to be straightforward principles are actually intertwined and inseparable issues. If each topic affects every other topic, do we end up in a vicious circle with no guidance about what to do? I do not think so. I said earlier that one of the advantages of contractualism is the flexible nature of the principles of intergenerational ethics that it produced. In my view it is actually a positive attribute that the principles governing each of these topics are flexible enough to respond to the different conditions caused by the others.

Recurring Themes

There have been several themes and key arguments that have appeared throughout and served to tie together the various topics in the book.

Moral Status of Future People

The most important theme that has lurked under almost every chapter is that ultimately current and future people are fundamentally of equal moral importance and ought not to be treated differently from each other. The fact that future people do not coexist with current people was found to be morally unimportant since the disanalogous properties (asymmetry of power, lack of reciprocity, lack of affective ties) that spring from non-overlapping generations were irrelevant within the contractualist framework. Since contractualism does not rely on any of these conditions, the same justification is owed to both groups in the same way, and there are no reasons to favour either group over the other. There have been some practical considerations that needed to be taken into account to maintain this point of view. This was especially true in Chapter 4, where I discussed what an appropriate response would be if current people were unable to achieve sufficiency for future people without sacrificing their own. I argued there that they could prioritize their own interests. However, this is consistent with the belief that both groups are owed equal consideration. Because current people are the only effective 'agents' when it comes to intergenerational ethics, and because under contractualism agents are permitted to give extra weight to their own interests, letting current people do so does not equate to claiming that current people are more morally important than future people. Theoretically, if it were possible for future people to prioritize their own interests (now), that would also be morally permissible. However, due to the procession of time, it is not. Furthermore, they will be entitled to do so once they are born, and so this is compatible with moral equality and impartiality even now.

Indeed, it is because current and future people are fundamentally equal that this book has wider relevance than just intergenerational relations. The point of this work has been to show that contractualism can accommodate future people, but also to discuss some issues that are particular to the intergenerational realm. Some of the principles that arose pertained solely to our relations to future people, like procreation and population size. But several principles I've defended could be just as easily applied *intra*generationally, and potentially even as a theory of global justice. The book has taken one group of people (current people) and discussed what obligations that group has towards another, equally important group (future people). Nothing precludes using exactly the same structure to consider what one group of people owes to a different group of people. For example, most of Chapter 3 could be a theory of global justice by substituting 'rich countries' for 'current people' and 'poor countries' for 'future people', and we would end up with a theory of global obligations that said that rich countries must provide poor countries with at least sufficiently good lives unless doing so forces them to forgo sufficiently good lives themselves, and so on. In addition, parts of Chapter 6, in particular the discussion of reasonable risk imposition, also have wider relevance among contemporaries. Therefore, although the aim of the book has been to consider the intergenerational context, some of the findings can be easily translated to and contribute to debates about justice among contemporaries including domestic global justice. They may also help us resolve the problem of how to balance the claims of future people against those of the currently existing poor.[1]

There is one final point to make clear about the equal status of current and future people. Throughout the book, I have implicitly assumed that it is current people deciding what to do for future people, but the principles I described are principles of *intergenerational* ethics, meaning that they also apply to future people. Most of the time, it is indeed current people deciding how to act with respect to future people. However, and mainly in the context of

---

[1] Elizabeth Finneron-Burns (2023), "Global Justice, Sovereign Wealth Funds, and Saving for the Future," *Critical Review of International Social and Political Philosophy*.

resource distribution, that there could be situations in which the principles require future people to make sacrifices for us, which is possible despite 'time's arrow' through mechanisms like deficit spending, for example. In this type of case, current governments would run deficit budgets (spending more than they take in through taxing current people) to pay for goods and services that benefit current people with the understanding that the debts would be paid off by future people. This is, in effect, borrowing from the future and could be a way in which future people make sacrifices for current people. This is not to say that it is always permissible for governments to overspend, but if it were determined that future people are required to make sacrifices for current people, there are ways in which it is possible to do so, and it is justified by the equal moral status of both groups.

Moral Status of Possible People

Another important theme has been the moral status of possible people. I argued more generally that a person's existence (or non-existence) was inadmissible in the contractualist framework. This meant that a 'person's' non-existence could not be a reason for rejecting a principle and that the fact that a principle caused someone to exist was a reason to justify the principle to that person. The latter was a key part of my response to the non-identity problem, and the former was tantamount to excluding possible people from the realm of those to whom we owe justification.

The fact that possible people are not owed justification also played a key part in many of the arguments of Chapters 4 and 5. It was important in explaining why we have no obligation to create the repugnant-sized population, but also that what is wrong with human extinction is its effects on current people and not because it prevents future people from existing. The fact that a person could reasonably reject a principle that left them with a bad (although worth-living) life played an important role in explaining why *Bad Lives* was not reasonably rejectable. Namely, a current person could not justify creating the child with the very bad life by saying, 'Because you exist with a worth-living life, there can be no objection to what I did, even though you have a very painful disease as a result.' The fact that the principle created *that child* does not preclude the person with a very bad life rejecting the principle on the grounds of the negative aspects of their life.

Balance and Strength of Reasons

A final important component was the development of a reason-balanced sufficientarianism and in particular the need to balance current and future people's reasons. One of the benefits of the contractualist method that I identified is its ability to accommodate varying circumstances and contexts. Some of the principles I addressed (for example, Savulescu's *Procreative Beneficence*) were intended to be universally applied. However, applying the same principle in all cases sometimes led to unintuitive results because it did not sufficiently take into account the circumstances of each agent. Contractualist principles, on the other hand, offered us the opportunity to consider the benefits and burdens for both the actor(s) and the person/people who would be affected by a principle when deciding whether or not it could be reasonably rejected. This means that non-rejectable principles are flexible enough to accommodate a number of different situations, and lead to more intuitive ideas about what is or is not permissible.

One way in which the balance of reasons was particularly important was with respect to the role of a sufficiency threshold, which appeared throughout the book. Rather than being a defined and rigidly adhered-to line above which we do one thing and below which we do another, its role was primarily to help signpost the strength of various parties' reasons. People below the sufficiency level have very strong reasons to want assistance, whereas those already above it have weaker reasons. This does not mean that they are owed nothing; rather, it means that the claims of the assistor need not be as strong in order to justify failing to assist. Once the strength of different parties' reasons was established, partly by their distance from the threshold, these reasons were then balanced against each other in the usual contractualist manner.

Risk and Uncertainty

Finally, the issue of risk and uncertainty came up in all three substantive topics (resource distribution, procreative choices, and population size). Most of the time when we act, and especially when we are considering the effects of our actions in the distant future, we are uncertain what the outcomes will be. In the discussion of procreation, the uncertainty was in the context of potentially passing on particular disease or disability traits to children. With respect to resource conservation, the problem was how to know what effect our conservation decisions would have on future people, and in particular, how to know how much or what type of resources they would need in order to lead sufficiently good lives. After discussing Scanlon's conception of reasonable risk imposition more generally, I then applied it to both cases. I argued that when it was undetermined what the likelihood of a bad outcome was, the actor must take the precautions that are reasonable and determined by both the probability and severity of the bad outcome.

Final Thoughts

Although there remain some opportunities for future research, this book has taken the step towards developing a contractualist theory of intergenerational moral obligations. It has sketched several principles that ought to govern the way we relate to the future in terms of procreation, resource conservation, and population size. What it has not done is set out every possible principle of intergenerational obligations that might apply. However, as the purpose was to defend the method through structural analysis and the plausibility of principles, this is not a problem. It has taken a general method of determining the permissibility of principles and highlighted the relevant constraints that must be taken into account in the particular case of future generations. The book showed this method to be sound, and it can therefore be applied to topics that involve future people that were not explicitly addressed in the book.

Bibliography

Agnafors, Marcus (2014). "The Harm Argument Against Surrogacy Revisited: Two Versions Not to Forget." *Medicine, Health and Philosophy* 17.

Althorpe, Caleb, and Elizabeth Finneron-Burns (forthcoming). "Are Saviour Siblings a Special Case in Procreative Ethics?" *Journal of Ethics and Social Philosophy*.

Anderson, Michelle J. (2016). "Marital Rape Laws Globally." In *Marital Rape: Consent, Marriage, and Social Change in Global Context*, ed. Kersti Yllo and M. Gabriella Torres (Oxford University Press).

Arneson, Richard (2005). "Distributive Justice and Basic Capability Equality." In *Capabilities Equality: Basic Issues and Problems*, ed. Alexander Kaufman (Routledge).

Arrhenius, Gustaf, Krister Bykvist, Tim Campbell, and Elizabeth Finneron-Burns, eds. (2022). *The Oxford Handbook of Population Ethics* (Oxford University Press).

Ashford, Elizabeth (2003). "The Demandingness of Scanlon's Contractualism." *Ethics* 113(2).

Barry, Brian (1991). *Essays in Political Theory: Liberty and Justice*, vol. 2 (Clarendon Press).

Benatar, David (2006). *Better Never to Have Been: The Harm of Coming into Existence* (Clarendon Press).

Broome, John (2004). *Weighing Lives* (Oxford University Press).

Caney, Simon (2021). "Climate Justice." In *The Stanford Encyclopedia of Philosophy*, ed. Edward N. Zalta (Stanford University Press.)

Casal, Paula (2007). "Why Sufficiency Is Not Enough." *Ethics* 117(2).

Christensen, James, Tom Parr, and David V. Axelsen (2022). "Justice for Millionaires?" *Economics & Philosophy* 38(3).

Clifton, Owen, and Rahul Kumar (in preparation). "Should Contractualists Be Longtermists?"

Conly, Sarah (2015). *One Child: Do We Have a Right to More?* (Oxford University Press).

Crisp, Roger (2003). "Equality, Priority, and Compassion." *Ethics* 113(4).

Dasgupta, Aisha and Partha Dasgupta (2022). "Population Overshoot." In *The Oxford Handbook of Population Ethics*, ed. Gustaf Arrhenius, Krister Bykvist, Tim Campbell, and Elizabeth Finneron-Burns (Oxford University Press).

de-Shalit, Avner (1995). *Why Posterity Matters: Environmental Policies and Future Generations* (Routledge).
Dey, Judith G., and Charles R. Pierret (2014). "Independence for Young Millennials: Moving Out and Boomeranging Back." *Monthly Labor Review*, U.S. Bureau of Labor Statistics.
Dor Yeshorim Centre for Jewish Genetics (n.d.). http://www.jewishgenetics.org/dor-yeshorim (accessed May 27, 2022).
Dorsey, Dale (2008). "Towards a Theory of the Basic Minimum." *Politics, Philosophy & Economics* 7(4).
English, Jane (1977). "Justice Between Generations." *Philosophical Studies* 31(2).
Fabre, Cécile (2007). *Justice in a Changing World* (Polity).
Feinberg, Joel (1986). "Wrongful Life and the Counterfactual Element in Harming." *Social Philosophy and Policy* 4.
Finneron-Burns, Elizabeth (2016). "Contractualism and the Non-Identity Problem." *Ethical Theory and Moral Practice* 19(5).
Finneron-Burns, Elizabeth (2017). "What's Wrong with Human Extinction?" *Canadian Journal of Philosophy* 47(2–3).
Finneron-Burns, Elizabeth (2018). "The Intergenerational Original Position." *Social Theory & Practice* 43(4).
Finneron-Burns, Elizabeth (2023). "Global Justice, Sovereign Wealth Funds, and Saving for the Future." *Critical Review of International Social and Political Philosophy.* Online First.
Finneron-Burns, Elizabeth (2022). "Human Extinction and Moral Worthwhileness." *Utilitas* 34(1).
Finneron-Burns, Elizabeth (forthcoming). "Humanity: Constitution, Value, and Extinction." *The Monist*.
Fotion, N., and Jan Christian Heller (1997). *Contingent Future Persons: On the Ethics of Deciding Who Will Live, or Not, in the Future* (Kluwer Academic Publishers).
Frankfurt, Henry (1987). "Equality as a Moral Ideal." *Ethics* 98(1).
Gardiner, Stephen (2009). "A Contract on Future Generations." In *Intergenerational Justice*, ed. Axel Gosseries and Lukas Meyer (Oxford University Press).
Gheaus, Anca (2019). "More Co-Parents, Fewer Children: Multiparenting and Sustainable Population." *Essays in Philosophy* 20(1).
Glover, Jonathan (2006). *Choosing Children: Genes, Disability, and Design* (Oxford University Press).
Golombok, Susan, et al. (2011). "Families Created Through Surrogacy: Mother-Child Relationships and Children's Psychological Adjustment at Age 7." *Developmental Psychology* 47(6).
Goodin, Robert E. (1985). "Vulnerabilities and Responsibilities: An Ethical Defense of the Welfare State." *American Political Science Review* 79(3).

Gordon, Robert J. (2012). "Is US Economic Growth Over? Faltering Innovation Confronts the Six Headwinds." National Bureau for Economic Research, Cambridge MA.

Gosseries, Axel (2009). "Three Models of Intergenerational Reciprocity." In *Intergenerational Justice*, ed. Axel Gosseries and Lukas Meyer (Oxford University Press).

Graley, Clare, Katherine May, and David McCoy (2011). "Postcode Lotteries in Public Health—The NHS Health Checks Programme in North West London." *BMC Public Health* 11.

Greaves, Hilary (2022). "Optimum Population Size." In *The Oxford Handbook of Population Ethics*, ed. Gustaf Arrhenius, Krister Bykvist, Tim Campbell, and Elizabeth Finneron-Burns (Oxford University Press).

Greaves, Hilary, and William MacAskill (2021). "The Case for Strong Longtermism." Global Priorities Institute Working Paper, University of Oxford.

Hare, R. M. (1973). "Rawls' Theory of Justice II." *Philosophical Quarterly* 23(92).

Harman, Elizabeth (2004). "Can We Harm and Benefit in Creating?" *Philosophical Perspectives* 1.

Heyd, David (1992). *Genethics: Moral Issues in the Creation of People* (University of California Press).

Hieronymi, Pamela (2011). "Of Metaethics and Motivation: The Appeal of Contractualism." In *Reasons and Recognition: Essays on the Philosophy of T. M. Scanlon*, ed. R. J. Wallace, Rahul Kumar, and Samuel Richard Freeman (Oxford University Press).

Holtug, Nils (2007). "On Giving Priority to Possible Future People." In *Hommage à Wlodek: 60 Philosophical Papers Dedicated to Wlodek Rabinowicz*, ed. T. Ronnow-Rasmussen et al. (Lund University).

Holtug, Nils (2010). *Persons, Interests, and Justice* (Oxford University Press).

Hubin, D. Clayton (1976). "Justice and Future Generations." *Philosophy & Public Affairs* 6(1).

Intergovernmental Panel on Climate Change (2022). "Climate Change 2022: Impacts, Adaptation, and Vulnerability."

Invitae (n.d.). "Deeper Genetic Insights." https://invitae.com/en/test-catalog/ (accessed May 27, 2022).

James, Aaron (2012). "Contractualism's (Not So) Slippery Slope." *Legal Theory* 18(3).

James, P. D. (2006). *The Children of Men* (Random House).

Kaczmarek, Patrick, and SJ Beard (2020). "Human Extinction and Our Obligations to the Past." *Utilitas* 32(2).

Kamm, Frances (1992). *Creation and Abortion: A Study in Moral and Legal Philosophy* (Oxford University Press).

Kavka, Gregory (1975). "Rawls on Total and Average Utilitarianism." *Philosophical Studies* 27(4).

Kavka, Gregory (1982). "The Paradox of Future Individuals." *Philosophy & Public Affairs* 11(2).

Kumar, Rahul (2009). "Wronging Future People." In *Intergenerational Justice*, ed. Axel Gosseries and Lukas Meyer (Oxford University Press).

Kumar, Rahul (2011). "Contractualism on the Shoal of Aggregation." In *Reasons and Recognition: Essays on the Philosophy of T. M. Scanlon*, ed. R. J. Wallace, Rahul Kumar, and Samuel Freeman (Oxford University Press).

Kumar, Rahul (2015). "Risking and Wronging." *Philosophy & Public Affairs* 43(1).

Lenman, James (2008). "Contractualism and Risk Imposition." *Politics, Philosophy & Economics* 7(1).

Levenbook, Barbara Baum (1984). "Harming Someone After His Death." *Ethics* 94(3).

MacAskill, William (2022). *What We Owe the Future* (Basic Books).

McMahan, Jeff (2009). "Asymmetries in the Morality of Causing People to Exist." In *Harming Future Persons: Ethics, Genetics and the Non-Identity Problem*, ed. Melinda A. Roberts and David Wasserman (Springer).

de Melo-Martín, Inmaculada (2004). "On Our Obligation to Select the Best Children: A Reply to Savulescu." *Bioethics* 18(1).

Mill, J. S. (1863). *Utilitarianism*. In *Mill: Utilitarianism and Other Essays*, ed. Mary Warnock (Collins).

Mills, Claudia (2005). "Are There Morally Problematic Reasons for Having Children?" *Philosophy & Public Policy Quarterly* 25(4).

Moore, G. E. (1903). *Principia Ethica* (Cambridge University Press).

Mounk, Yascha (2012). "An Interview with T. M. Scanlon (Part I)." *The Utopian* (blog), https://www.the-utopian.org/T.M.-Scanlon-Interview-1.

Mulgan, Tim (2006). *Future People: A Moderate Consequentialist Account of Our Obligations to Future Generations* (Clarendon Press).

National Organization for Rare Diseases (n.d.) https://rarediseases.org/rare-diseases/tay-sachs-disease/ (accessed June 14, 2022).

National Tay Sachs and Allied Diseases Association (n.d.). http://www.tay-sachs.org (accessed May 27, 2022).

Neumayer, Eric (2003). *Weak Versus Strong Sustainability: Exploring the Limits of Two Opposing Paradigms* (Edward Elgar).

Nevada Colorado River Commission (2002). "World Fossil Fuel Reserves and Projected Depletion." https://ca1-mcb.edcdn.com/documents/world-fossil-reserves.pdf?mtime=20160408065525.

Norges Bank Investment Management (n.d.). "Fund Size Projection." http://www.nbim.no/en/the-fund/market-value/forecast-for-the-size-of-the-fund-/ (accessed May 2, 2022).

Norges Bank Investment Management (n.d.). "The Fund." http://www.nbim.no/en/the-fund (accessed May 2, 2022).

BIBLIOGRAPHY 211

Office of National Statistics (2020). "Childbearing for Women in England and Wales: 2019." https://www.ons.gov.uk/peoplepopulationandcommunity/birthsdeathsandmarriages/conceptionandfertilityrates/bulletins/childbearingforwomenbornindifferentyearsenglandandwales/2019.

O'Neill, John (1993). "Future Generations: Present Harms." *Philosophy* 68(263).

O'Neill, Martin (2008). "What Should Egalitarians Believe?" *Philosophy & Public Affairs* 36(2).

O'Neill, Martin (2013). "Constructing a Contractualist Egalitarianism: Equality After Scanlon." *Journal of Moral Philosophy* 10(4).

Ord, Toby (2020). *The Precipice: Existential Risk and the Future of Humanity* (Bloomsbury).

Ortiz-Ospina, Esteban, and Max Roser (2017). "Happiness and Life Satisfaction." Our World in Data. https://ourworldindata.org/happiness-and-life-satisfaction.

Page, Edward (2007). "Justice Between Generations: Investigating a Sufficientarian Approach." *Journal of Global Ethics* 3(1).

Parfit, Derek (1984). *Reasons and Persons* (Clarendon Press).

Parfit, Derek (2000). "Equality or Priority?" In *The Ideal of Equality*, ed. Matthew Clayton and Andrew Williams (Palgrave).

Parfit, Derek (2011). *On What Matters*, vol. 2 (Oxford University Press).

Partridge, Ernest (1976). "Rawls and the Duty to Posterity." PhD thesis, University of Utah.

Rawls, John (1971). *A Theory of Justice* (Belknap Press of Harvard University Press).

Rawls, John (1999). *A Theory of Justice*, rev. ed. (Belknap Press of Harvard University Press).

Rawls, John (2005). *Political Liberalism* (Columbia University Press).

Reiman, John (2007). "Being Fair to Future People: The Non-Identity Problem in the Original Position." *Philosophy & Public Affairs* 35(1).

Richards, David (1971). *A Theory of Reasons for Action* (Oxford University Press).

Ridge, Michael (2001). "Saving Scanlon: Contractualism and Agent-Relativity." *Journal of Political Philosophy* 9.

Roberts, Melinda A. (1998). *Child Versus Childmaker: Future Persons and Present Duties in Ethics and the Law* (Rowman & Littlefield).

Roberts, Melinda A. (2010). *Abortion and the Moral Significance of Merely Possible Persons* (Springer).

Rulli, Tina (2016). "Preferring a Genetically-Related Child." *Journal of Moral Philosophy* 13.

Ryberg, Jesper (1996). "Is the Repugnant Conclusion Repugnant?" *Philosophical Papers* 25.

Savulescu, Julian (2001). "Procreative Beneficence: Why We Should Select the Best Children." *Bioethics* 15(5–6).
Scanlon, T. M. (1982). "Contractualism and Utilitarianism." In *Utilitarianism and Beyond*, ed. Amartya Sen and Bernard Williams (Cambridge University Press).
Scanlon, T. M. (1998). *What We Owe to Each Other* (Belknap Press of Harvard University Press).
Scanlon, T. M. (2004a). "Replies." In *On What We Owe to Each Other*, ed. Philip Stratton-Lake (Blackwell Press).
Scanlon, T. M. (2004b). "When Does Equality Matter?" John F. Kennedy School of Government, Harvard University, Cambridge, MA.
Scanlon, T. M. (2007). "Wrongness and Reasons: A Reexamination." *Oxford Studies in Metaethics* 2.
Scanlon, T. M. (2018). *Why Does Inequality Matter?* (Oxford University Press).
Scheffler, Samuel (2012). *Death and the Afterlife* (Oxford University Press).
Secretariat of the Convention on Biological Diversity (2010). "Third Global Biodiversity Outlook." Convention on Biological Diversity, Montreal.
Segall, Shlomi (2015). "Incas and Aliens: The Truth in Telic Egalitarianism." *Economics and Philosophy* 32.
Shields, Liam (2016). *Just Enough* (Edinburgh University Press).
Sidgwick, Henry (1874). *The Methods of Ethics* (Macmillan).
Singer, Peter (1993). *Practical Ethics*, 2nd ed. (Cambridge University Press).
Singer, Peter, Nick Beckstead, and Matt Wage (2013). "Preventing Human Extinction." *Effective Altruism* (blog), https://forum.effectivealtruism.org/posts/tXoE6wrEQv7GoDivb/preventing-human-extinction.
Sinnot-Armstrong, Walter (2006). *Moral Skepticisms* (Oxford University Press).
Southwood, Nicholas (2010). *Contractualism and the Foundations of Morality* (Oxford University Press).
Spina Bifida Association (n.d.). http://www.spinabifidaassociation.org/.
Spina Bifida Association (n.d.). "Folic Acid." https://www.spinabifidaassociation.org/resource/folic-acid/#-pbcJump.
Statistics Canada (2016). "Life Expectancy." http://www.statcan.gc.ca/pub/82-229-x/2009001/demo/lif-eng.htm.
Steinbock, Bonnie (1986). "The Logical Case for Wrongful Life." *Hastings Center Report* 16.
Stern, Nicholas (2010). "The Economics of Climate Change." In *Climate Ethics: Essential Readings*, ed. Stephen Gardiner, Simon Caney, Dale Jamieson, and Henry Shue (Oxford University Press).
Stratton-Lake, Philip (2003). "Scanlon's Contractualism and the Redundancy Objection." *Analysis* 63(277).
Suikkanen, Jussi (2005). "Contractualist Replies to the Redundancy Objections." *Theoria* 71(1).

Tännsjö, Torbjörn (2002). "Why We Ought to Accept the Repugnant Conclusion." *Utilitas* 14(3).
Temkin, Larry (2003). "Egalitarianism Defended." *Ethics* 113(4).
United Nations (2004). "Population to 2300." Department of Economic and Social Affairs, United Nations, New York.
Weinberg, Rivka (2008). "Identifying and Dissolving the Non-Identity Problem." *Philosophical Studies* 137(1).
Weinberg, Rivka (2015). *The Risk of a Lifetime* (Oxford University Press).
Wenar, Leif (2003). "What We Owe to Distant Others." *Politics, Philosophy & Economics* 2(3).
West, J. Jason (2013). "Co-Benefits of Mitigating Global Greenhouse Gas Emissions for Future Air Quality and Human Health." *Nature Climate Change* 3(10).
Woodward, James (1986). "The Non-Identity Problem." *Ethics* 96(4).
Wynes, Seth, and Kimberly A. Nicholas (2017). "The Climate Mitigation Gap: Education and Government Recommendations Miss the Most Effective Individual Actions." *Environmental Research Letters* 12.
Zimmerman, Eilene (2013). "The Race to a $100 Genome." CNN Money, http://money.cnn.com/2013/06/25/technology/enterprise/low-cost-genome-sequencing/.
Zuber, Stéphane et al. (2021). "What Should We Agree on About the Repugnant Conclusion?" *Utilitas* 33.

Index

For the benefit of digital users, indexed terms that span two pages (e.g., 52–53) may, on occasion, appear on only one of those pages.

Additional Resources, 119, 120, 194
admissible reasons, 53–54, 62–69, 73, 76–77, 161
appeal of contractualism, 52–54

Bad Lives
    definition of, 131
    our future is uncertain and, 176–77
    permissible procreation and, 130–36
    Reasonable Risk and, 176–77
    what *do* we owe to future people and, 183–84, 186–87
Barry, Brian, 1, 25–26
Beckstead, Nick, 143
Benatar, David, 84–85
birthright principles, 126–28

Children of Men, The (James), 150
climate change, 1, 98–99, 140, 148–49, 177–78, 191–94
complaint model of contractualism, 70, 80–85
Constraint Principle (CP), 28–29
content problem
    contractualism and, 13–14, 53
    definition of, 3–4
    non-identity problem and, 6–11
    optimal population size and, 11–13
    overview of, 3–4
contractualism
    appeal of, 52–54
    circularity claims against, 43–44n.50
    complaint model of, 70
    content problem and, 13–14, 53
    human extinction and, 37–38
    justification to future people and, 55
    nature of contract in, 15
    non-identity problem and, 30–34
    overview of, 13–14
    procreative principles and, 128–39
    Rawls's contractualism, 15–39
    reasonable rejection and, 42–43, 45–46, 47–49
    reasons and reasonableness and, 41–47
    relation between Rawls and Scanlon on, 15, 40
    Scanlon's contractualism, 40–54
    scope problem and, 13–14, 15, 50–52

Depletion/Conservation, 79–86
disanalogies between inter- and intragenerational context, 56–60
distribution of resources. *See* intergenerational resource distribution

egalitarianism. *See* intergenerational egalitarianism
extinction. *See* human extinction

Free Procreation, 122–23
future people. *See* intergenerational ethics overview; justification to future people; what do we owe to future people

Gardiner, Stephen, 28–29, 143
Goodin, Robert, 133–34
Good Lives
  definition of, 138
  permissible procreation and, 136–39
  what *do* we owe to future people and, 184–85, 189

Hare, R. M., 26–27
Helpfulness, 109, 118, 137
Hubin, Don, 23–24, 29
human extinction
  contractualism and, 37–38
  implications for the permissibility of, 153–56
  loss of intelligent life, civilization, and progress and, 145–46
  Obligatory Creation and, 150–52
  pain and death and, 146–49
  preventing life and, 142–45
  psychological pain and, 149–50
  risk of, 197–98

Insufficient Resources, 118, 120
interest in existing, 73–77
intergenerational egalitarianism
  reason-balanced sufficientarianism and, 107–13
  Scanlon's reasons to object to inequality, 90–96
  sufficientarianism, 101–7
  telic egalitarianism and, 96–101
intergenerational ethics overview. *See also* what do we owe to future people
  balance and strength of reasons, 204–5
  challenges posed by intergenerational ethics, 1
  climate change, 1
  content problem, 3–4
  COVID-19 pandemic, 2
  currency, 3–4
  definition of intergenerational ethics, 2
  moral status of future people, 201–3
  moral status of possible people, 203–4
  non-identity problem and, 6–11
  practical importance of intergenerational ethics, 1
  repugnant conclusion, 11–13
  risk and uncertainty, 205
  scope problem, 3–4
intergenerational resource distribution
  Additional Resources and, 120
  content and justification for, 88–89
  control and, 92–93
  egalitarianism and, 90–101
  equal concern and, 94–95
  Insufficient Resources and, 118, 120
  levelling-down objection and, 99–100
  methodology for, 90–107
  opportunity provided through, 88–89, 93–94
  political fairness and, 93–94
  procedural fairness and, 94
  Scanlon's reasons to object to inequality and, 90–96
  sufficientarianism and, 101–7
  Sufficient Resources and, 114–18
  telic egalitarianism and, 96–101
  unfair economic institutions and, 95–96
Intergovernmental Panel on Climate Change's (IPCC) Sixth Assessment Report (AR6), 191–92

justification to future people
  admissible reasons and, 63–69
  complaint model and, 80–85
  contractualism and, 55
  Depletion/Conservation
    and, 79–86
  disanalogous properties
    and, 56–60
  including future people
    and, 60–63
  interest in existing and, 73–77
  Kumar's solution to the non-
    identity problem and, 71–77
  moral motivation and, 57
  non-identity problem and, 69–87
  non-welfare related
    reasons and, 65–69
  scope problem and, 57
  trustee model and, 60–62
  welfare reasons and, 63–65
just savings principle
  argument, 16–19

Kumar, Rahul, 71–77

levelling-down objection, 99–100
lives not worth living, 38
longtermism, 197–98
loss of intelligent life, civilization,
  and progress, 145–46

McMahan, Jeff, 79, 144–45
Mulgan, Tim, 12–13, 37–38, 55, 157

non-identity problem (NIP)
  assumptions of, 10–11
  challenge posed by, 9–10
  complaint model and, 80–85
  content problem and, 6–11
  contractualism and, 30–34
  definition of, 7
  different people choice and, 8
  examples of, 7–8
  interest in existing and, 73–77

justification to future people
  and, 69–87
Kumar's solution to, 71–77
lack of accepted solution to, 10–11
overview of, 6–11
present time of entry assumption
  and, 30–31
same people choice and, 7–8
scope problem and, 6–11
time-dependence claim and, 6–7
non-intrinsic egalitarianism, 90–96
not intending to parent, 188–89
numbers of future
  generations, 180–82

Obligatory Creation, 150–52
obligatory repugnance, 160–61
O'Neill, Martin, 94–95, 143
optimal population size
  content problem and, 11–13
  human extinction and, 13, 142–56
  loss of intelligent life, civilization,
    and progress and, 145–46
  no optimal population
    size, 165–66
  Obligatory Creation and, 150–52
  obligatory repugnance
    and, 160–61
  permissible repugnance
    and, 161–65
  preventing life and, 142–45
  repugnant conclusion and, 11–13,
    141–42, 156–65
  scope problem and, 11–13
  total utilitarianism and, 11

Parfit, Derek
  complaint model and, 80–82
  contractualism and, 32–33, 35–
    37, 70n.8
  Depletion/Conservation example
    of, 79–86
  non-identity problem and,
    6, 80–81

Parfit, Derek (*cont.*)
   repugnant conclusion and, 11–13, 157
   telic egalitarianism and, 96–97
Partridge, Ernest, 23, 35
permissible procreation
   Bad Lives and, 130–36
   birthright principles and, 126–28
   contractualist procreative principles for, 128–39
   Free Procreation and, 122–23
   Good Lives and, 136–39
   Helpfulness and, 137
   old, unhappy, or oppressed procreation, 184–87
   parental motivation and, 129–30
   parental responsibilities and, 133–34
   potential governing principles for, 122–28
   poverty and, 186–88
   Procreative Balance and, 128–30
   Procreative Beneficence and, 123–26, 128
   Rescue and, 130, 137
   saviour siblings, 189–91
   sufficient threshold and, 126–28
permissible repugnance, 161–65
population policies, 195–96
population size. *See* optimal population size
present time of entry (PTE) interpretation, 16–35
preventing life, 142–45
procreation. *See* optimal population size; permissible procreation
Procreative Balance, 128–30
Procreative Beneficence, 123–26, 128
psychological pain, 149–50
present time of entry interpretation, 16–35

Rawls, John
   aim of contract for, 16
   altered motivation assumption and, 22–26
   alternative interpretation and, 35–39
   atemporal interpretation of membership configuration and, 26–35
   conceivability of possible people and, 37
   Constraint Principle (CP) and, 28–29
   contractualism of, 15–39
   intergenerational ethics and, 1, 16–19, 22–23
   just savings principle argument and, 16–19
   limitations of contractualism of, 15, 39
   lives not worth living and, 38
   membership configuration for original position and, 20–39
   non-identity problem and, 30–34
   original formulation of membership configuration and, 21–26
   original position and, 16–18
   parties as representatives and, 29–30, 33–36
   present time of entry assumption and, 16–35
   rationality described by, 41
   reformulation of ideas of, 28–29
   Scanlon's contractualism and, 15, 40
   scope problem and, 15
Reasonable Risk, 174, 176–77
reasons and reasonableness, 41–47
representatives, 29–30, 33–36
repugnant conclusion
   definition of, 12

obligatory repugnance and, 160–61
optimal population size and, 11–13, 141–42, 156–65
permissible repugnance and, 161–65
populations A and Z and, 158–65
Rescue, 108, 109, 130, 137
resource distribution. *See* intergenerational resource distribution
Roberts, Melinda, 37, 122–23
Rulli, Tina, 134–35

saviour siblings, 189–91
Savulescu, Julian, 123–26
Scanlon, T.M.
  admissible reasons and, 63
  appeal of contractualism and, 52–54
  contractualism of, 40–54
  generic constraint on reasons and, 46–47
  Helpfulness and, 109
  individual constraint on reasons and, 43–44
  justifiability and, 53
  justifiability to all possible people and, 74
  marginal cases and, 51
  nature of contract for, 40
  non-identity problem and, 70
  non-intrinsic egalitarianism of, 90–96
  personal constraint on reasons and, 44–46
  Rawl's contractualism and, 15, 40
  reasonable rejection and, 42, 47–49, 67–68, 70, 107–9
  reasons and reasonableness and, 41–47
  reasons to object to inequality, 90–96
  Rescue and, 108–9
  scope problem and, 50–52, 57–60
  trustees model and, 50n.55
Scheffler, Samuel, 149–50
scope problem
  asymmetry between present and future people and, 5
  challenges for, 4–13
  contractualism and, 13–14, 15, 50–52
  justification to future people and, 57
  lack of existence of future people and, 4–5
  non-identity problem and, 6–11
  optimal population size and, 11–13
  overview of, 3–4
  scope-as-agents, 50–51
  scope-as-sphere, 50–51
  time-dependence claim and, 6–7
Segall, Shlomi, 97–98
Shields, Liam, 109–10
Singer, Peter, 115, 143
size of population. *See* optimal population size
sufficientarianism
  disproportionality and, 103
  indifference above the threshold and, 104
  prioritarianism and, 112–13
  reason-balanced sufficientarianism, 107–13
  shift thesis and, 109–10
  sufficient resources principle and, 114–18
  upward transfers and, 103–4
Sufficient Resources, 114–18, 181

Tannsjö, Torbjörn, 158–59
telic egalitarianism, 96–101
Temkin, Larry, 100
trustee model, 60–62

uncertainty about the future
   Bad Lives and, 176–77
   future people's needs and, 177–80
   numbers of future generations and, 180–82
   risk and, 167–77

Wage, Matt, 143
Weinberg, Rivka, 75, 82, 126, 128–30, 188
Why Does Inequality Matter? (Scanlon), 90
Woodward, James, 48–49, 83–84